JAN

D0752991

SOC

GENERATION
Queer

BOB PARIS

GENERATION
Queer

A GAY MAN'S QUEST FOR HOPE, LOVE, AND JUSTICE

3 1336 04976 1787

WARNER BOOKS

A Time Warner Company

If you purchase this book without a cover you should be aware that this book may have been stolen property and reported as "unsold and destroyed" to the publisher. In such case neither the author nor the publisher has received any payment for this "stripped book."

Copyright © 1998 by Bob Paris
All rights reserved.

Warner Books, Inc. 1271 Avenue of the Americas, New York, NY 10020
Visit our Website at www.warnerbooks.com

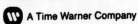 A Time Warner Company

Printed in the United States of America

First Trade Printing: June 1999

10 9 8 7 6 5 4 3 2 1

The Library of Congress has cataloged the hardcover edition as follows:

Library of Congress Cataloging-in-Publication Data

Paris, Bob.
Generation queer : a gay man's quest for hope, love, and justice /
Bob Paris.
p. cm.
ISBN 0-446-52275-9
1. Paris, Bob. 2. Gay men — United States — Biography. 3. Self-esteem in men — United States. I. Title.
HQ75.8.P37 1998
305.38'9664'092 — dc21
[B]   97-51218
                                                    CIP

ISBN: 0-446-67535-0 (pbk.)

Cover design by Carolyn Lechter

ATTENTION: SCHOOLS AND CORPORATIONS
WARNER books are available at quantity discounts with bulk purchase for educational, business, or sales promotional use. For information, please write to: SPECIAL SALES DEPARTMENT, WARNER BOOKS, 1271 AVENUE OF THE AMERICAS, NEW YORK, NY. 10020

For Brian, with love

ACKNOWLEDGMENTS

Many thanks to Basil Kane, Diane Stockwell and John Aherne for their work on behalf of this book.

We are not to be praised for doing our share;
we are only to be blamed for not doing it.

Jacqueline Bouvier Kennedy

PART
ONE

1

STAND UP AND DIVE UNDER

I want to tell you a secret; it's not my only secret, but it's a strong one nonetheless. No. On second thought, better take first things first by stating the obvious. I am a queer man. That's certainly no secret. It's not everything I am, but it is certainly an important part of who I am. The secret I want to tell you, however, is directly related to my being queer.

So what's this big secret of mine? It's this: each day, on some level, I must come to grips with the fact that being gay makes me feel both wonderfully gifted and painfully cursed, and—more importantly—that both of these extremes come from inside me and nowhere else.

Every time I begin to feel smug, or think that I've accomplished all the growth necessary for this lifetime, something comes around to remind me that my work toward becoming a more fully evolved human spirit still continues. I could easily say that I've done all my homework, that I've healed every hurt, that I love myself fully, and unconditionally accept the queer part of myself, but those statements would eventually reveal themselves as—at the very least—partial lies. I could also say that I've totally accepted the gifts that my gayness has brought to my life, but that would also be only partly true. I know that in my own life, even with as much conscious work as I've done and as much as my queerness appears to be lived with unwavering pride, there is still so much further to go. Sometimes I feel as if I've worn the leather off the bottoms of a dozen pairs of shoes making this trip. But whenever I begin to feel that way I remind myself that the journey is more important than the destination.

But I have made some progress in that I no longer fear admitting that I'm not all the way there yet. I've begun to understand: acknowledging I'm still learning isn't an admission of weakness, but a sign of developing maturity. So many in the public eye—especially activists—seem scared to admit that they still have more work to do toward greater self-acceptance, fearing perhaps that ever-vigilant critics will seize upon this honesty as a declaration of total self-hate, as if self-

love and self-hate were always clear-cut, easily catego-
rized, two-dimensional issues. I choose to actively set
aside those fears, and with all my heart encourage others to do the same. For me, this whole gay thing revolves so much around the personal struggle toward
deeper, higher self-respect—anyone else's analysis of
where I am in my growth fades in comparison to how
I view my own progress on the road toward pure, unconditional self-love.

So I live each day with these feelings that seem so
diametrically opposed: the gift and the curse. And I
wonder how to keep going in the face of these difficult
challenges laid on my doorstep. It would be so simple
to lash out at the world and pin all of my pain and frustrations on outside sources. But if I did that, wouldn't
I also have to credit all the good stuff, all the positive
accomplishments, to things outside myself as well?
That just doesn't hold up to my experience. I create
who I am. At the deepest level, who I view myself as
being is who I wind up being. No matter how much I
might blame the world around me, it always comes
right back to it being my personal responsibility if I really want to become the most evolved human being
that I can possibly be.

Now, don't get me wrong; feeling gifted or cursed
is very definitely influenced by outside factors, but in

the end, it all comes down to me: my perceptions, my reactions, my traumas, my triumphs, my fears, my joys. And I don't believe that this is the type of issue that's limited to me, or to gay people. There is no monopoly on self-pity here. We tell ourselves lies when we believe that our hurts are greater than anyone else's.

Let me tell you another thing, which is secret to some, well known to others. We are—all of us—simultaneously as different as night and day, and shockingly the same. Most of us tend to pay stronger attention to the former than the latter, especially when times get tough. You know—the way people who have everything in the world to like about each other can sometimes hate each other's guts instead, indulging in the meanest, lowest twists of animal fear.

Let me give you an example: an activist buddy of mine told me that at a meeting a few months ago, another activist (they were both on the same board of directors for one good cause or another) stood up and called him a self-hating queer, simply because they'd disagreed on how to spend some money that was going to go to the right place no matter which man's vision was followed. The second activist started calling my friend a right-wing Nazi and all sorts of other nonsense. They yelled back and forth at each other and within a few minutes the meeting broke up and nothing much was accomplished. I know both of these men, one much better than the other, but I know them; both their hearts are good. In essence they want the same things. Peel away all the petty details, the feverish disagreements, the hiding behind issues and names, and you'd most likely find a core concern. They both just want to be treated right. They both want a fair place in the world to be themselves, completely themselves.

Heaven seeks us. Until we are ready, we resist.

. . .

I am queer, a faggot. Coming from some lips those words are an insult, from others a compliment. I will always be a queer. Always have been. It's who I was made to be, or at least one aspect of who I was made to be.

I have a lot in common with all the non-queers in society. Just like them, I was taught from the earliest age I can remember to despise anything to do with homosexuality. There aren't too many people living in our society who can truthfully claim otherwise. Most of us learned those early lessons very well; we believed the old myths, and even when every ounce of evidence proved the myths lies, they continued as threads woven through the fabric of our lives. That's what we have to get at: the root of those lies and the way they can continue to wrap around the place where our soul and mind come together. It isn't enough to go around acting proud. Sure, it's important, but hardly enough. You've got to get at what boils underneath. Go right into the heart of the lie and replace it with truth.

I constantly remind myself that I deserve to be here. Whenever I begin to feel self-doubt, I look to the lies I was told about who I grew up to be. They aren't the root in every case, but a lot of times it's those lies and false myths rearing their nasty heads that make me act in a less than loving way. Self-hate and self-love fight for control of our rational and spiritual lives for as long as we draw breath. Acknowledging that fact is more than half the battle.

．．．

I make a big deal out of being queer, because to not make a big deal means a lifetime of pain. People who don't even know my name—who don't even think about the fact that I came out of a mother's womb, was enfolded by a grandma's arms, and was filled with spirit by the same higher power they were—hate me for the simple fact that I am queer. And most of them actually have the audacity to claim that it isn't hate. All these years I have believed that Jesus preached against hypocrisy. But see, now I catch myself easily slipping into blaming others. Yes, Jesus preached against hypocrisy, but he also taught that Heaven rests inside each one of us. I must be vigilant enough to spot my own stumbles into hypocrisy, stumbles that keep me disconnected. I can be angry, but if I don't want to be hated, I must turn my back on hatred first. That back-turning is a struggle seemingly without end.

Let's face it, it could be argued that queers have every reason in the world to hate those who condemn them. In the eyes of those who hate queers "just be-cause," we are sinners bound for the everlasting pits of fire and damnation. That's quite a burden to carry around throughout a lifetime. So I do everything I can to not hold it against them—the ones who hate me "just because." I try my best not to hate them back anymore. Instead, I feel sorry for them, for a simple reason: there is no way for the human heart to hold such naked, overwhelming hate and pure love—the pure love that wise spiritual teachers have always spo-ken of—at the same time. They are inversions of sameness, but cannot occupy the same space. So I work hard to not hate those who hate me and that is a difficult battle. Bigots can't be happy, I tell myself. Spiritual evolution and hatred cannot coexist. So I try hard to feel the way one would hope that—in a perfect world—those who carry so much judgment and hardness in their hearts would eventually learn to feel about people different from themselves. I feel compassion. I feel forgiveness. I do not for one instant, however, feel forgetful. Or disconnected. Or complacent. Bigotry only has the power to harm me if I participate in it. My mission in life is not to make everyone like me, but rather to remove myself—at root level—from the participation in illusion. If—in my deepest subconscious—I give antigay bigotry weight in my life, it must be because some part of me still believes the lies. That's why I must go deep inside myself, to try to find the source of any hardness I hold. What are the hurts and hatreds that still linger down inside the place where my heart, mind, and soul intersect? What things inside of me still need more loving attention?

* * *

I live on an island now. With my boyfriend. A glorious man of full consciousness and good spirit whom I want to marry and live the rest of my life with. And we live on an island in the Northwest; so northwest, in fact, that Canada lies but ten miles from our house. We tried the city. There was nothing wrong with it, except for the fact that we both wanted to wake up every morning and walk out into the wet, cool woods holding hands and sipping coffee, in the woods at the edge of cerulean water surfing over purple and gold starfish and crashing on boulders. We shared this dream of nature. It's one of the things that brought us together in the first place, drew me toward him. There was also this quality about his green eyes, the way I saw the goddess of beauty and a February desert moon reflected in them. And his freckled Irish skin. And I fantasized right away about what it would be like to wake up to Brian's morning breath and wild hair, in a double sleeping bag next to the ocean.

I lived on what has now become our island for almost two years, alone, before I met him. The foundations of my life had gone through dramatic changes and I went there to regroup, to regain my personal and spiritual perspective. A nipple of the earth—that's what I called that giant rock sticking up out of the ocean. A spiritual talisman that I could walk on.

For some, the island would be the perfect description of hell; isolated, underpopulated, subprovincial, quiet. For me and Brian it's a pure slice of Heaven.

Somewhat contrary to my fundamentalist religious upbringing and my later (seemingly mandatory) New Age spiritual education, I do not see Heaven as perfect—at least not perfect in the way humans tend to envision perfection. That is, I do not view it as being problem free or without challenge. Everyone sees it differently—Heaven. Some hear harps, others anticipate the black silence of nothing. I'm starting to think that Heaven is a lot like life. We find whatever we expect.

. . .

The grain of life is entropic. It wants to pull us down in a spiral. We stand up. That alone is an exhausting battle. Beyond that, we fight against the downpull, or turn our backs and ignore it, out of exhaustion. It is in fighting against the natural downward spiral of life that we become strong and whole and literally uplifted. Gravity teaches us lessons; we are silly to ignore them. As a gay man, I have learned that these figurative battles against gravity are among the greatest gifts the world has laid before me. The gift of my queerness has contained the invaluable lesson of learning to grow stronger by opposing the currents in the river of unconscious tradition. I've learned that the grain of life wants us to stand up against its natural forces and that, in standing up and continuing on and on past exhaustion, we find the depth of our being, the strength of our fullest humanity. For this reason alone (and there are many others besides), I thank the heavens for making me queer. I thank the heavens for planting me here, in this wondrous time of change and challenge, among these generations of fighters standing up against gravity and seeking Heaven.

. . .

I became an activist pretty much without having to think about it. I crossed a line and—wham—next thing I knew I was talking about gay rights (and by extension, racism, sexism, and a bunch of other -isms) in front of thousands of people at a time, all over the country. I was suddenly telling strangers how I'd learned to live a good, fulfilling life in the face of sometimes unrelenting adversity. It was an earthshaking transition for me. I fought the gravity, which whispered in my ear, constantly—"Go back to safety, you've done your share, this is too hard"—and kept going at it for nearly six years. Only in the last couple of years, as I purposefully withdrew from public speaking, have I had enough energy to take a breath and gather some perspective on what it all has meant and what I'd learned from the experience.

Even though I had been politically active from an early age, at the time when I crossed the line—when I said the words in a magazine article, "I am gay"—I was not on a traditional activist track. But is there really any such thing as a traditional path for activists? Probably not. People reach a crossroads in life, for some reason see

a need for change or justice or both, and get involved—
sometimes overwhelmed—to the point of near drowning, but are rescued by passion. Others can have nearly
identical experiences and turn away. Some choose to
stay, others walk on. All I know is that there were so
many times when I was sure that I was drowning or that
my stomach would burst from pain, but I kept going,
even while being roundly slaughtered by some of the
very people who I thought were on the same side—other
queers; even when my opinions weren't popular; even
when I got little or no credit, or was written off as irrelevant because of how I looked or the field from which I'd
come into my activism. I've thought everything through
for the past few years, and the path was the right one. A
journey into the farthest, coldest waters of tested faith, so
that I could learn both who I was and who I was not.
Like most people I am only able to see the route in reverse, as I look back behind me and piece together
where I've been. Now I realize—fully—what has been
dawning on me for years. We make a choice each day
what kind of person we will be, what kind of world, nation, and community we will help create.

. . .

Brian and I were sitting out on the front porch the
other night, wrapped in each other's arms, watching

the sunset. An eagle was spiraling on wind currents out over the water. An elderly couple—man and woman, both with brilliant shining white hair and proud walks—hiked up the gravel road arm in arm and waved. We waved back. They came up the path toward the house, right to the edge of the porch where we sat, and the four of us talked about the weather and the summer's huge yellow jacket population and so on. They looked at us sitting there still wrapped together and I thought I could see in their eyes memories of how they had been when they were our age. They joined us on the porch and we sat silently until the light was gone.

All differences had fallen away and we were simply dancing spirits, fighting against the gravity of life, on a big rock in the middle of the ocean, finding Heaven in a moment.

■ ■ ■

I started out wanting to tell a different story. It wasn't exactly a nice one either, although I had managed to convince myself that it was necessary. It was a story colored by revenge. Settling scores. Venting pent-up anger. It wasn't even directed at any one person or group, or anything particularly concrete. It was anger and tiredness and frustration, which were all actually pointing the way to areas where I needed more work. When it finally got down to it, the approach of lashing out with an angry voice revealed itself to be nonsense, a short-term fix. Trying to even old scores tends to only expand the initial problem, and revenge is contagious: it grows exponentially until all space is filled with its putrid air. So I leave that behind and strive instead for a path of greater joy and love. That's where I want my voice to come from. So I begin on a different path of words and strive only to be fully, authentically myself.

■ ■ ■

The island I live on is a place separated from the mainland by miles of swirling, deceptively dangerous, cold ocean water. A person living in this place generally travels by ferry to go to and from America (as the locals refer to the mainland).

A couple of years ago I read in a small local paper an article intended to inform tourists about the place where I live. It was a humorous piece about the silliest questions workers on the ferries had been asked by tourists, things such as: Are the islands here all year around? One question of the bunch, however, stuck out. Are the islands connected under the water? a woman had reportedly asked a ferry crew member.

What a stupid question, I initially thought. And I laughed at how silly tourists could be, as if the laughter could prevent me from remembering what it felt like to be a stranger in unfamiliar surroundings. How easy it is to slip into cynicism, ridiculing the other, the stranger, the outsider, laughing to make ourselves feel better about our own unsure footing. How easy to poke fun and miss the point. How simple it is to grow smug and protective.

Are the islands connected under the water? The question still rolls around the back of my head and I have to laugh at myself for initially leaping past the obvious and therefore missing the subtle: of course the islands are connected under the water. You just have to break the surface and go a distance down to really see how much they're connected, and how much more they are connected to than just each other.

To be fully human, we must simultaneously fight against gravity and go beneath the surface. It is possible. It requires stretching and persistence and the willingness to sometimes have our sacred cows sacrificed in the name of unfolding wisdom.

In seeking Heaven we should not forget that the

islands of our lives are connected under the rough and frigid waters of separation and difference.

·   ·   ·

Let me tell you a secret. I have a wish that infiltrates my prayers every morning and night. I wish that instead of always searching for differences—the things that set us apart—more people would look beneath the surface and see how connected we all truly are. Our differences are not reasons for hatred and fear, but gravity which we all struggle against in order to be fully human, to remind ourselves why we are here. To find Heaven we must go deeper and reach higher, stand up and dive under.

2

FAITH: LOST AND FOUND

I needed to write this book as a reminder to myself. Conventional wisdom has always instructed writers to tell stories about what we know. So that's what I'll do. I come here humbly, to share hard-earned insights. I am neither here to tell anyone how to live nor to create a new fundamentalism of the one ultimate way to be a real queer. I simply pass along observations that rise out of my own experience, hoping that I may be reminded of the lessons and that in writing about these issues, I might influence others to see reflections that seem true.

I have had to learn in order to know what to say here. My own personal path to this place of understanding has not been smooth. I used to think that one day life would lighten up and get easier, but instead it seems to fill in from beneath. Remove one rock and another seems to pop into its place, but I keep on trying to fill my wheelbarrow and move the pile.

I need to hear these words now, so that I can remember what the point was of crossing the line, of sharing information that in a more enlightened world would merit a "so what?" And really, isn't being queer something of a "so what?" issue? At its simplest level, it should be. The problem is that, although our gayness is a small part of who we are, we still live in a world that makes it into a big deal.

We get to "so what?" by telling our stories, by revealing our secrets and letting the world know that we are here and aren't going away. To move forward, into a world where all of the old, false assumptions are distant memories, we must constantly tell our stories to the people around us. Doing so may be the only way we can make others understand. It is certainly one of the only ways to understand ourselves. Telling our stories and talking through our issues deflates the myths and old lies.

Every time you cross the line, telling someone in your life about your experience as a gay person, you have participated in important activism. Our collective mission is to replace the old rocks of false myth with newer, stronger rocks of proud self-declaration.

Stand up and be counted. Take the scattered rocks in life's field and build a solid stone wall, build two walls, create a temple of celebration.

What must it be like to live a life where there are no lines to cross, where the line doesn't seem to present itself every time you're buying groceries with your boyfriend or telling your grandma, in a completely honest way, about how your life's going. I'm never sure if the non-gay people in my life ever fully grasp what it's like to constantly have to take a stand, or hate yourself when you choose not to; what it's like to be forced to either make some sort of a statement or pretend to not hear a complete stranger ask you if your lover is your brother or cousin or roommate. Will the family I was born into ever really understand the wounds sliced across the gay heart, cuts created out of false myths and lies, arteries severed from being told that we could never simultaneously be ourselves and happy? And will the scars from wounds made so early on— way back in boyhood—ever fade completely, or will they stay with me as if I'd been mutilated by a bad car wreck in the days before plastic surgery?

Why does it feel as if we have to keep fighting the same battles over and over? Because to do otherwise would be to surrender a war that we are already winning. When will the changes finally take hold? They already are. I believe that in my lifetime we will see a full evolution take place. The evidence is far too clear. Like a long, low-grade earthquake, the ground beneath us has been shifting for some time now, altered in ways that we will only be able to fully appreciate with time and perspective. Our struggle is like a vast pointillist painting. Up close we only see the blur of different colored paint dots. But if we take a few steps back those dots—which looked so separate and unrelated before—both melt and sharpen into a full picture. Together, through each of our individual actions, we are creating our collective pointillist painting and must remember that the dots of color will—and already do—add up to something. We must be patient and persistent enough not to lose courage while waiting for the dots to come together.

In the meantime, the earth is still rumbling and the work must continue. I, for one, need to keep reminding myself that although we may be winning this war, the battles are far from over. There are a lot of us who suffer battle fatigue and don't remember what any other sort of life was like. I need to ignore my tiredness, my impatience with how slow the process feels, and stop reading defeat in every minor setback. If I am to encourage others to continue on, or to engage more fully in the cause, I must also keep going. Sure, I have

other choices, but none of them will satisfy my con-
science, or my sense of personal and generational responsibility.

. . .

I must stop to breathe now. For years, seemingly forever, my life was caught up in such intense activism
that the public fight seemed to take over every waking
moment and more than a few sleeping ones as well.
Everything else in life faded into lesser priorities. Even
when I was in my real career, competing as a professional in my sport, not an instant passed when I didn't,
at some level, say to myself: I am gay and an activist for
my community. Every action was soaked by that. But
now all that has begun to shift.

    I ask myself, what has all this process and struggle
for justice meant? What does someone gain when
every effort feels like a sacrifice, when income dimin-
ishes, or the upward arc of a career seems stalled by
honesty, or when privacy is surrendered because there
is such a need to speak out and tell the stories? I can't
help wondering what my life would have been like if,
instead of publicly coming out in the media, I had
simply continued living life as the quietly "out" man
that I was before the change. Where are the boundaries? How far do we each need to go to create the shift

toward justice and true equality? After all, I wasn't exactly a closet case. I was completely out to my family and friends, out in my work. Everyone knew that I was gay; the men I dated were generally integrated into my life. Why then that change, which put my life on such a different path for so many years? The one reasonable answer that I keep coming up with is that, by taking such a public stand, I gained a level of self-respect that may have taken years—perhaps decades—longer to achieve otherwise.

I've read in some of the gay papers how I'd become an activist for the money. Now there's a bizarre concept. It would be hilarious if the accusation didn't sting so much, if it didn't fall so far off the mark. I remember asking myself every time I'd see cynical comments such as that, ones that were such misinterpretations of my personal motives, why, in the face of such severe misunderstanding, I kept going.

And then I would remember: a young gay man who was an All-American baseball player kicked off his Big Ten team just for being queer; the coach willing to sacrifice wins so that his team wouldn't be polluted by a fag. A minister run out of her small town for daring to show up at a church function with her girlfriend. The teenagers thinking of suicide, older men and women describing the hell their lives had been in earlier, less tolerant decades, and on and on. The stories people told me; the letters that had come in by the tens of thousands. The question of why would fade some when I remembered those stories.

. . .

I say a prayer. It is a prayer of understanding. I ask God to show me how to put it all into perspective, all those things that confuse me, my questions of why and how come and what it all means.

> *Infinite Spirit,*
> *Show me the way. Help me to see and understand*
> *the things that confuse me. I give thanks for the*
> *beauty in my life. I thank You, God, for Your gifts.*
> *Allow Your highest divine plan to continue un-*
> *folding in my life, with grace and in a perfect*
> *way. Allow my heart to always turn toward love.*
> *Help me to remember Your pure love. Allow me to*
> *see who I truly am, so that I may see Your spirit in*
> *others. Amen.*

I was half-heartedly saying this one particular prayer on an early morning last May, repeating it, but not really paying attention, as if it were background music. I was by myself, deep in the wood behind the house, walking up a steep hill—with a lot of worries on my mind—when I came upon three deer grazing at the edge of the trail, a shaft of early sun shining on them like a klieg light. The sight made me gasp and click back from my distraction to the beauty at hand. I'd been feeling blue and lonely. Brian, this man whom I had grown to love so much—so passionately—was still living more than a thousand miles away and I had come to the island to get the house ready for him to move in. We were going to be apart for nearly a month, and because of that we were both feeling miserable, but overjoyed at the same time— the separation meant that our lives were moving toward being together, living the life we both had always dreamed of. He was coming up as soon as he wrapped up his work responsibilities, but that wasn't fast enough, so I was walking in the woods feeling lonely, longing for him, praying for insight and understanding. And I came upon three deer eating in the sunlight. I suddenly remembered why it was all worth it, and thought that everything in my life seemed to lead me to this trail, on this morning, to these deer. I sat down on the ground and gave thanks to God for everything: the good and the bad, challenges, frustrations and joys, everything. I thanked Him for leading me here and for giving me the ability to see how much I had to be grateful for.

. . .

I believe in God. I turned my back on my faith for a good, long while because of how I was brought up. Funny how that works. I was raised in a very religious family, but had to lose my faith to really find it. After all, how could I continue to believe in a system of worship that supposedly said that just because I was gay, God would make me writhe and burn in flames forever and ever without end? The God of my youth seemed cruel and vindictive, the ultimate skinhead, fag-basher; I take them into paradise, but not you. And who needs that? But the power that guides our lives doesn't just disappear because we turn our backs.

. . .

I am already in trouble, in quicksand—at least with some—because I address the taboo. Not only that, but I also speak of what can barely be put into words. When I say "God," I do so realizing that I am in over my head and using the tiny box of language to communicate a concept that is different to every believer. By "God," I do not mean an old guy with a white beard and a long white robe. I speak of the power governing our lives. When I think of God, I see neither man nor woman, young nor old, white nor black—nothing that mirrors our physical limitations and language. My words fall short; replace them with your own favorites, since we most likely speak of the same thing. In my own prayers I call God by many names, depending upon my mood: Infinite Power or Spirit, Goddess, Jesus, and so on. To me, they each mean the same thing. Substance—in matters spiritual—is always more important than style.

■ ■ ■

But that's not the only rule I've violated; I speak of what is supposed to be off-limits to me, both as a queer and as a thinking person. When you're queer, according to the cynics, belief in anything even remotely spiritual is against the rules, stupid and hopelessly naive. Spirituality is unwanted by "real" queers. Everyone's entitled to his or her opinion, but I attempt to offer a contradiction to that cynical notion. Queer men and women are far more spiritually in tune than anyone would like to believe. We show it in our worship and we show it in our nihilism, two sides of the same coin. As queers—and supposed outsiders in most things conventionally religious—we actually have to think about what the concept of God means, not just attach ourselves to ancient stories, repeated like mantras of certitude. We must fight to establish a true, heartfelt dialogue with the holder of the strings. And eventually, as we go through the process of letting go of the old myths, we grow closer to God than we could have ever imagined being. We find the place where worn-out dogma disappears. We discover the truth in the stories that say even Jesus was a rebel against the fundamentalists of his time, which is one of the key things fundamentalists of our time conveniently forget, ignore, or misinterpret.

Like most others living in Judeo-Christian America, I was brought up to believe that God was a sort of anthropomorphic super-being off in the clouds and that He had this tremendously advanced X-ray vision enabling Him to watch, record, judge, and condemn my every move. In more cynical times, I used the style of my early religious upbringing to justify ignoring the substance of its core spiritual message, but not anymore. Myths, such as the white-bearded, vengeful God, came from people attempting to put into identifiable terms what was felt, but not necessarily seen. It was in that same style of ancient myth building—stories passed from campfire to campfire—that all of the lies about who people like me are blossomed and thrived. And they thrived until the ones the myths were told about found enough inspiration—enough of God—to stand up and say, that's a lie. I am proof that myths are lies. And God loves me too, by the way.

So when I talk about God (and my spiritual beliefs color nearly everything in my life), I do so with respect for all of our different pictures and names. I know that there is a divine power guiding my life, because every time I've been brought to my knees in grief, every time I've felt tragedy, every time I've looked at the ocean and had my breath taken away, I've felt that power well up inside my heart. Infinite Spirit is real, and more of us believe that than either fundamentalist religion-ists or fundamentalist cynics want to admit. I see this power as emanating from inside each one of us; it is the thing that brings people together in tragedy, the concept that compels us to try to make our society a better place for those who come after us. It is the power of pure love. It's the power that persuades many of us to strive to live ethical lives and fight so hard for justice.

So I gladly violate the rules by humbly but vigorously dipping my toes into the waters of the divine. I have the right to do so. So do you. The powers that put us here in this place, in this time, are here and they are real. I violate the rules and say that queers have the right to claim the infinite too.

When we reclaim our true and honest spirits, our hearts open like the Grand Canyon and the mystical truly enters.

. . .

It is time to live our lives differently. In many ways, both large and small, many of us have already begun doing this. We search. We try to find ways to break free of the limits that the cynics and jaundiced cultural watchdogs, inside and outside the gay community, tell us are our only birthright.

A very wise, non-gay friend of mine says that he greatly admires the gay community's ongoing battle for respect, and that he tries to model his life on the lessons of hope and positive reinvention that he has learned from his queer family and friends. He claims that his spirit has evolved in dramatic and positive ways by watching the gay people in his life fight to establish a legitimate foothold in a world that usually gives no consideration at all to the queer. Whether we realize it or not, we are demonstrating to the world a strong model for how to create a new and bold way of living, a way that fights the tide of unconscious acceptance of worn-out rules. We have had to look at life and say that the limits lie far beyond where we are now. We have had to listen to others tell us where the boundaries are. Be careful in believing anyone who tells you what your limits are. My experience has generally been that the messengers of doom reveal their own limitations and tell us that—if we have any intelligence whatsoever—their limits also must be ours, so that they don't wail in darkness alone.

We have everything in the world to celebrate. At no other time in the known history of this planet have queer citizens experienced so much positive change so rapidly. Say a prayer of thanks for that. It has been hard won. This fight is not over, but there is no way to turn the clock back. And yet we must not grow complacent, we must not hesitate, we must continue. We must pray for strength.

. . .

When the mystical enters, our surroundings become completely irrelevant. We can be in the busiest city or on the most remote farm, but when it happens, when we turn around and understand that those who use God to condemn us are more lost than we ever thought we could be, when we see that we have more gifts than we ever imagined, then the magic of our lives can truly begin. Let the cynics call us fools, the self-proclaimed saved call us sinners; that's nothing except fear speaking through the mouths of the scared.

And we must turn our backs on fear. To do that we must, without apology or hesitation, turn our hearts toward love—love of others and more than anything else love for ourselves. We have everything in the world to love about ourselves. The mission is: start now. Take everything you've ever been taught about who you are and begin to filter it through your heart. If your heart is hard (and given everything that most outsiders must fight against, who wouldn't have to fight to keep their heart soft and warm?) begin today to turn it around. Today is the day.

. . .

I never thought I'd love again, but in the end, rational thinking had very little to do with it. I couldn't think my way back into loving again. I had to live my life in such a way that a new understanding of love would grow from seeds inside my heart. I had to live as if the shift had already happened, as if I deserved love, before I could truly experience it.

I had buckled under the weight of a crushed heart. There was no true blame to be laid; two lives had come together and then pulled apart. I was wounded though, and for a time, thought that hardheartedness was the only answer. But then I made a choice. I would heal my heart and not allow it to turn to granite. I never wanted to be someone who experiences the shift out of romantic partnership and, in reaction, becomes one who sneers. If something in my life—no matter what it was—didn't last as long as my heart or head had wanted it to, that did not mean that an entire concept was impossible, or undesirable; it meant that I had experienced the torture of unpreventable change. But it went beyond that. I was once again reminded that inside every painful experience lie the seeds of hope, if only I have the courage to look at the situation for what it really is. From the moment I knew that the course of my life had irretrievably shifted, I worked to turn my heart inward, toward itself, and that changed everything. I found my own personal intensive care unit, the one that ran truest for me and me only (the forests and beaches of my island), and I set about having a healing love affair with my own wounded heart.

Through using the hardship as an opportunity for growth, I felt reborn. And as with all birth, the pain was great and I thought that the labor would never pass. I began lost, with no map or compass, but along the way rediscovered my belief in ultimate perfection of divine will, my trust in that piece of highest power that intertwines inside us all. I had truly begun another leg of the journey toward my most authentic self.

I never thought I would love again, never thought I'd
see the world as a beautiful place. But I had misjudged
my capacity for healing and renewal. I had been sidetracked from my long-held belief that all love begins at
home. It seemed as if tragedy was there to remind me
that the soul's growth never ends. The lessons keep on
coming right up to the last breath.)

. . .

(I remember the day and hour of my own change of
heart. I was sitting alone, in my new home, simultaneously allowing my mind to race around the haunted cas-
tle of bitterness and hating myself for the indulgence.
With each moment my spirit sank lower, sliding toward
a major depression. I recall suddenly stopping in mid-
thought and telling myself that I didn't want to go
there. So I did what I usually try to do when my mind
heads in such a negative direction. I breathed myself
down into a quiet mental space, got my thoughts to slow
down and began to pray for guidance. By the time I'd
finished praying, the bitterness of disappointment was at
least dissipated and in its place was a different, although
anything but new, realization: To have love, we must be
loving. To fully experience the love of another, we must
begin and sustain a love affair with the mystical and
wondrous self we each are born to be. Nothing outside

of our own loving hearts will provide us with the true healing we require. We must first stand up and truthfully tell ourselves our own story—tell it with compassion and honesty—and then set about soothing and comforting the wounds gathered along the way.

In seeking Heaven we must remember that the hardest part of all is truly believing—in our heart of hearts—that we deserve to be there. Once that's conquered, Heaven surrounds us and all that we touch, even during tragedy.⟩

• • •

When I came across three deer feeding in the woods, it hit me. I had so much to be grateful for. I was able to live where I wanted and love who I wanted. I gave a prayer of thanks for all the warriors of peace who came before me, who enabled me to live this life, who laid the bricks on the path toward justice. I forgave myself a bit for being so down. I reminded myself that my separation from the one I loved would not last forever, and soon the time would pass. And here I was, after so many years of struggling toward self-acceptance, taking for granted the ability to live as an openly gay man in one of the most remote places in the country. I gave thanks for the fact that I was finally understanding that the only walls that held me in were self-created, and that those same confining walls could be—stone by stone—disassembled and rebuilt into a temple of celebration. I was thankful that I live in a time when people like me no longer feel bound, either psychologically or physically, to live in one of the three or four neighborhoods in the nation where they perceive themselves to be free, truly themselves; former limited assumptions always compelled us to move to those easy boxes, ghettos. Within reason, at this junction of history, I could be who I wanted, where I wanted. Even the old ghettos had begun to feel free of long-defended assumptions, with people living there more because they wanted to than because they had to.

. . .

It wasn't perfect yet. No, far from it; I wasn't naive enough to believe that there wouldn't be more struggles, but I had the strength to say, to perceived enemies and disgruntled allies alike, I have the right to be here too and if you don't like it, tough. Given my own uphill battle toward self-respect, that, in and of itself, was a major personal victory. The change had begun a whole new chapter; it continued whether I wanted it to or not, and there was no going back. I couldn't ignore it, because even if I tried, something would come around to remind me of both how far I'd come and how much further there was to go.

3

GENERATION QUEER

Infinite Spirit,
Allow me to see my surroundings through the eyes
of love. I ask that Your strength fill my heart, so
that I am able to better understand. Help me,
God, to be thankful for those who came before
me, who paved the way so that I could live with a
greater sense of freedom. Help me also to remem-
ber those who will follow me on this path of life.
Let me always remember what it was like for me.
Allow me to use those memories for the greater
good. Fill me with Your strength so that I will take
responsibility for positive change, so that I do my
share in assuring that those who follow may have
a better life. Help me to have the strength to do

my part in making this world a more just place for everyone. Amen.

. . .

It is easy to forget, when wrapped up in day-to-day life, that there was a time when things were very different. In our hunger for faster, greater movement forward, it can be so simple to forget how much has changed in a very short period. Once we have decided that resisting a particular change is futile, both individually and collectively human minds tend to swerve toward integrating shifts and quickly adapting, sometimes nearly to the point of amnesia. It always amazes me how many queers seem to forget, until somehow reminded, how hard their own growing up was and what a different world they now live in.

Maintaining gratitude for the changes that have taken place is not a passive process. Gratitude is active, living. It must be constantly reinforced and watered. Otherwise we might forget how far we've come and— in forgetting—lose our way.

. . .

I live on the cusp between the two generations of what can loosely be called modern-day American queerdom:

the two generations now so fashionably called Baby Boomers and Generation Xers. At the age of thirty-seven, I am not fully one or the other, but instead feel bookended by the sometimes divergent world views of those several years older and younger. A creature of the gulf am I, and that gulf can be vast—so vast that ignoring it can seem simpler than facing its contradictions: the place where difference fades and similarities and commonalities come racing together. I grew up—as I imagine we all did—hearing all about the generation gap. It exists, but it also can be an illusion. And it's far easier, when you're nineteen and just coming out, to imagine that you have nothing at all in common with someone who is fifty, who may have lived as a queer in a vastly different culture. Or the other way around: a fifty year old imagining what it must be like for a fifteen year old today to be able to come out in high school.

Young versus old; it is a struggle as old as any we know. Perhaps it is a natural process: the new generation kicking the preceding one out of the way, wanting to run the show; the older generation questioning the sanity of the young. Whatever the reasons for this gap, beyond simple differences in life experience and historical perspective, there is much the generations can learn from each other. That may seem obvious in theory, but it seems to prove difficult, elusive, in practice.

If we truly went into the heart of this gap, however, we would see that there is an opportunity being presented here, one that transcends the naturally occurring gulf between the generations. It is another of the queer's opportunities to lead the way toward a new and more enlightened humanity. The illusion of there being an uncrossable, rock-strewn valley in between the generations can nearly disappear when we acknowledge the similar battles we all must wage for interior and exterior respect; being nineteen or fifty can seem identical when faced with the issues of moving to the flowing, ever-shifting rhythms of self-love and self-hate.

If we look, we will find so much to learn from each other's experience. If we look hard enough we will find so much to respect in each other that we will wonder what took us to long to realize it in the first place. From looking and really trying to understand each other, we can learn a level of human respect that climbs higher and dives deeper than we ever imagined possible. And agenda item number one in the struggle for equal rights must be respect. So many times, though, we look for respect to come to us from the outside before fully developing the self-respect. We must look inside. We must find that piece of our own humanity, our own soaring spirits, that craves the heights

and depths of true respect, and then, without flinch-
ing, look for those same things in others.

．　．　．

There are few elements in life as consistent as change.
Change will always happen, no matter how hard we
try to prevent it from occurring. Since it is inevitable,
change should be embraced and molded—or at least
interpreted—to our advantage. What worked yesterday
may not be as effective tomorrow. Strategies must be
adjusted, updated, and polished into plans of action
that work in a changing world. If we factor into our
lives the inevitability of change, anticipate it and ad-
just accordingly, learning from both past mistakes and
successes, we create an alchemist's recipe for even
greater success in the future. Acting upon the constantly changing dynamics of the world around us is
what keeps us fully alive. We need to be active right
here and right now, always with one eye on what will
work tomorrow. Instead of fearing the shifts in strategy
that are necessary for forward movement, we should
embrace them with acts of faith and constant action.
But most of all we must believe that we will get the
things that we go after—if we continue on a heartfelt
search for the most productive roads to our goals.

All anyone who doubts the need for adjusted

strategies in a changing world has to do is look at a
phenomenon—such as the ongoing queer civil rights
movement—to see that yesterday's approach needs
constant attention and adjustment. In the space of a
bit more than two generations, an evolution—a long,
low rumbling revolution—has taken place. The past is
a wondrous reminder, a place where we can return to
gather wisdom, but the past is gone; its circumstances
can never return. The world does not stand still. Remain caught in the past, and the movement stalls; prepare for the future and the cause moves forward.
Inside that fundamental concept lies one of the great
secrets of social justice. And, along with interior and
exterior respect, absolute social justice is exactly what
we should all be after. Those who would deny queers
justice in this society claim that we are pursuing special privileges, but there's nothing special or privileged
about simple social justice. It is our birthright, not because the Constitution or any other legislation says so,
but because it is part of a divine plan for full human
evolution.

One thing is certain: queer Americans deserve—
as their promised birthright as citizens—the full gamut
of absolute social justice, rights, and responsibilities. It
will take our full and continuing commitment to the
cause of justice to get where we need to be. It will take

all of us engaging in this battle, on a variety of fronts, to change the world. We cannot ever cede the responsibility to elements outside of ourselves. Anyone who believes that a shining knight on a white horse is going to take this issue by storm, and magically grant complete and universal social justice for all gay women and men, must realize that the only shining knight will be the concerted efforts of all people who believe that the issues revolving around full and nondiscriminatory citizenship are essential ingredients for a truly enlightened civilization. Granted, "everyone" is a monolithic term in this regard, and that monolith represents an extremely diverse group of people. When you have such a diverse group—many having sexuality as the only trait in common—all parties must continually find ways of setting differences aside in the interest of achieving a greater good. Common ground must be found and cultivated.

The pettiness of labels—conservative, effeminate, liberal, butch, single, monogamous, promiscuous, and so on—can not, must not, stand in the way of working toward common priorities and goals that move us toward a fully just society. To move toward that ideal we all must first acknowledge that even with all the progress the gay rights movement has achieved, the struggle still exists here and now, and the battle will still roll on into the future. Those with any role in this ongoing process must find ways to speak to each other, and set secondary issues aside, in order to keep moving toward justice.

. . .

We don't need to agree all the time. We can see things differently and still live in a peaceful world. Building that peace, however, takes more than just talk; it takes continued desire and action.

Talk without action is nothing but dirt cheap, virtual reality. It's like paddling a canoe from the safety of a distant armchair, like watching a nature show and claiming you've actually been to the Amazon, as you sit there with the TV remote in your hand and potato chip crumbs on your shirt.

At some point action is vital and unavoidable. But not every action must be identical to be of equal value.

. . .

Queers in this country have a historic opportunity, one that presents itself on social and spiritual fronts. We can demonstrate to the rest of the nation what it is like for such a diverse group of citizens—who sometimes have only one factor in common—to come together and reinvent their place in the world. We have the opportunity to reinvent our social discourse and our actions in such a dramatic and positive way that everyone else will eventually want to emulate our model. That reinvention is already happening. Others are already taking notice. We cannot grow tired and turn our backs. We must try harder, dig deeper, reach higher to find connection with each other. The time for talk has passed; we must acknowledge that our common experience demonstrates that. They—in slightly different shoes—are Us. It is time to see how alike we all are and stop viewing every human interaction from the perspective of difference.

. . .

We are no longer at a time when we can hold our desire for freedom and justice at bay. Those who would try to stand in the way can yell and scream all they want, but we cannot go backward. Perhaps we may experience setbacks, but even in setbacks we can find experiences that will lead to greater freedom. One usually learns as much, or more, from mistakes as from successes.

To experience freedom, though, we must be willing to fully accept the delicate balancing act between rights and responsibilities. There cannot be one without the other. The very notion of freedom conjures for some images of license, of being able to do anything at any time, without effect or consequence. The universe does not view this as justice or a high spiritual truth, but as selfishness and the opposite of true freedom; license is, for many, a jail cell. The freedom we seek lies deep within our own hearts and it is through the eradication of fear that our hearts move toward justice. It is less important to have our rights on paper than to believe—fully believe—with every ounce of our hearts that we all deserve to have equal rights. If we first set out to cure our hearts of this doubt—doubt built into our very upbringing by way of all the myths and lies each of us, to varying degrees, grew up with— then our collectively healing hearts, with more powerful, new beliefs constantly unfolding, will exert influence exponentially greater than we ever imagined possible. We heal our hearts through both belief and practice.

Begin by acting as if you have every right to be here and to be treated with equal justice, and then act upon and help reinforce those beliefs in others around you. We must constantly re-create the way we view the world, and above all else we must become examples of justice ourselves. We must be responsible. We must participate and be engaged—no one will do it for us. Every action counts.

We must become complete living, shining examples—warriors of peaceful change—standing up against the downward spiral. Act as if you have everything to believe in, to find hope in, to see light in; believe it with all your heart. With that action you change one life: your own. By changing that one all-important life, you will have an impact on everyone around you. Make yourself into someone you are proud to be. From this root change, every aspect of life will improve. Not because the unavoidable challenges and disappointments of life will come to a halt, but because your perspective will change; you will enable yourself to back away from the canvas and see how your dots of paint help make up a vital part of the whole picture.

Open your heart—your healing heart—and your dreams can unfold in magnificent ways. Dare to be fully yourself, full of life and uplifting energy. Dare to see the beauty in the hearts of others—even those you feel you have every right to hate.

Jesus said to love your enemies; he didn't say that we wouldn't have enemies, just that we should not hate them, but instead expose their injustices to them through loving means. There is no room in a loving heart for hatred. There is room for anger, and as outsiders, denied what is rightfully ours, we are entitled to our share of anger, but in filtering anger through love you become a warrior of peace.

. . .

There was a time, not too long ago, when I decided that I never ever again wanted to explicitly come out to another human being. I decided that I should simply live my life assuming that every person I encountered either knew that I was queer, or didn't care. I also decided to give everyone I encountered the benefit of the doubt and speak as if they weren't at all prejudiced against queers.

Quite simply, these thoughts grew out of being sick of explaining myself. I was tired of being a full-time homosexual example, some sort of an educator on gay issues for every Tom, Dick, or Mary who came down the road or crossed my path. I was sick of explaining to strangers—some gabby seatmate on an airplane, for example—things that were, in a perfect world, none of their business; responding—as if I were required—to everyday, chatty, mundane questions such as "Are you married?" "What does your wife do?" with my politically charged (even if gently stated) queer rights manifesto. I mean, why is this anyone's business? And why is it that the nature of even a casual conversation with a stranger seems to change when I say that I don't have a wife, and that I'm, in fact, gay? I know that this all sounds tinged with anger; when I used to have those encounters, I was angry. But was my anger displaced? Does the frustration come from something other than taking issue with the nosiness of a stranger? Is it organic in my nature? Would it stand alone in my personality if I weren't queer, if I hadn't gone through so many years of being uncomfortable with the disclosure of that information?

So I stop myself again and try to establish if I shouldn't take a different course, if I shouldn't interrupt the thought process that leads me toward impatience with these exchanges. I must step back and try to separate the apple from the seed. Perhaps there is something deeper here, something I'm missing or forgetting. I need to dig deeper, to fight the gravity and not take the easy way out.

. . .

I read once that if you write, you should erase your tracks, a blend of memories and experiences, and not reveal the process that got you to the finished product. In most cases I would agree; to do the contrary seems self-conscious: the painter talking about the canvas, instead of simply presenting the finished work. But I will be perfectly honest about my process here. I want to leave a few tracks, simply because my own personal path seems to be tied in to the recording of these thoughts. I am both author and participant, test tube and scientist.

Here is a footprint, an unerased track: When I began working on this project, I was going to talk for a couple of hundred pages about policy and legislation and the day-to-day battle of legal issues for gay men and women—all sorts of policy wonk stuff. But why? There certainly are dozens of other well-written, effective works that cover these areas of the struggle. I began on that course, but eventually, after several drafts in the wrong direction, landed on top of a different premise.

So, am I supposed to spend page after page saying that queers deserve to be treated right, with respect and equality? Would anyone be reading these words and not already believe that idea to be valid? Perhaps some, but certainly not most. So, without any further preamble, debate, or discussion, I will simply say that queers deserve equal rights in this society. I say this without apology, without attempting to explain away bigotry. We tend to do way too much explaining away of others' hatred of us. We must accept that the hatred makes no sense and come up with other ways to get to our common goals besides trying to get every antigay bigot in the country to set aside his or her ignorance and like us. They cannot make us worthy of anything. We are already inherently worthy. We deserve to be here and we deserve to be treated with equal regard, and we deserve to have all the rights of first class citizenship.

Imagine any minority group having to sit and explain away the irrational, fear-based prejudice of others under the disingenuous guise of equal time and balance. Isn't that what we, as queers, are always told? It seems as if any time one of us appears on a television or radio show, there always has to be a bigot there for supposed balance. Why? We must reject the notion that our enemies occupy equal moral ground.

I reject, out of hand, the notion—so commonly accepted as some sort of fact—that the Christian Bible condemns queers to everlasting Hell. God loves all of us; the energy of Infinite Spirit made us who we are, and so long as we treat each other with love and respect we live up to high moral principles and find Heaven.

There are tracks that I never want to erase, experiences that shape my words and thoughts, making me believe that to go further than any of us can even imagine, we must—while simultaneously working toward strong legislative goals—begin to believe that our truest work is right in the center of each of our individual hearts. Until we decide to truly, unflinchingly, honestly explore that territory, no amount of antidiscrimination legislation will completely soothe our collective pain. We have the ability to help lead the world toward light. We must each find the strength and hope and will; we must fight the gravity of indifference and decide to begin, to continue. I try my best not to erase the tracks that are truly important. Memories of pivotal events are tracks that lead me back in time to the point where I understood that I was queer and needed to deal with it. That I never wanted to forget. And it has always amazed me how many queers have tried to forget where they came from, the pain they have been through.

. . .

I live on the cusp and acknowledge the different perspectives of the generations that came before and the ones that came after. Each generation has its own set of general assumptions. But when you live, not just as a Boomer or a Gen Xer, but also as a part of the Generation Queer, you cannot afford to ignore the others who seem so different. Our common dialogue should be more about sameness than difference. We should be helping each other find Heaven, by holding up a light and turning our backs on the cold wind of separation.

. . .

When I first moved to the island where I now live, a friend gave me a book to read. It was a beautifully written, slim biography of an early white settler on the island. He and his wife had come west, at the turn of the century, searching out the farthest piece of land they could find, and they had landed on this island, which was still, for the most part, an uninhabited wilderness. They had been considered so queer—so oddly different—by the friends and loved ones they left behind, but they fought the odds, survived the storms and traumas, and made a life for themselves. They left behind, on this island, a homestead—which they'd hacked out of the raw woods and worked with their bare hands— for their children and their children's children; the generations that followed inherited the paradise that had so much of those original fingerprints on it.

If I walk out my front door, I can hike up through the woods along a ridge that overlooks that old homestead. As small farms on remote islands go, it is certainly paradise. And I feel grateful that those people—considered so queer by traditional societal norms—had come out here and paved the way. In the book, there are ancient fading photographs of the town where I now shop for groceries and pick up my mail. It was a thick forest with a couple of temporary looking buildings near the shore. What must this place have looked like to the first humans who saw it, long before these pictures were taken? I wondered. I think about this, how wildernesses can become habitable — how wilderness doesn't have to be destroyed to create a solid home — and compare it to my own life experience. I may have found an isolated place to live, but I did not have to clear a dense forest with an ax to make my way across it. Someone — many — had come before, leading the way to roads and towns and stores and churches and a way of life far less daunting than the pioneers had ever dreamed of.

Reading that book had started me thinking about my own life and the lives of those like me — the queers of the world, ones who began adrift with no recognizable landmarks, who made their way into the isolated regions of the heart in search of truth, of honest identity. I remembered a story I'd been told, not just by one man but by at least a half a dozen older gay men who'd lived in Greenwich Village, New York, in the 1940s and '50s. The telling of the story always grew out of a conversation about how the youngest members of Generation Queer had little understanding of what life was really like just a short time ago, and how easy it was for the young to take for granted the pioneering efforts of the old.

Each man's version of the story was always remarkably similar. You'd swear that you were encountering the queer version of the old "I walked ten miles to school through neck-deep snow" myth that so many of us heard growing up. But listening to each man tell this story, I believed him. The story wasn't long, but made up in revelation what it lacked in length. In the 1940s and '50s—in Greenwich Village of all places, which was even then one of the only "safe zones" for queers—there were a few places that were considered gay bars. Everyone knew them, even though their entrances were usually indistinct, nearly hidden, detectable mostly only by the radar—the gaydar—of those seeking them out. Inside these bars, human contact of any description was kept to a minimum. In fact, people would sit at the bar and have to look straight ahead, neither left nor right. Undercover cops roamed and if a man was caught *looking* at another man—not touching, mind you, not having sex, or dancing, or holding hands, but merely looking away from his gin and tonic in an indistinct direction, which could be read as looking at another man—he could, and very well might be, arrested. Every man who told me this story, or one similar, said that he always went to the bars with a

fifty or hundred dollar bill hidden in a sock, always prepared for the possibility of bribes or bail. You gambled
your entire life on seeking some connection.

Newspapers would print articles about raids on
"nests of fairies." Lives would be crushed by the scandal of being busted on a morals charge, branded for
life a pervert. Life was a horror if you were honest, a
horror if you lied.

. . .

Now, several years and quantum leaps later, we have
grown impatient with a planet, a nation, that would
have been an unrecognizable dimension to the 1940s
Greenwich Village queer. Kids come out in high
school, in junior high school, not just in big cities but
in small towns. Editorial pages of nearly every major
urban newspaper support gay issues at some level, at
least at a level unheard of ten, twenty, thirty years ago—
even if that support is simply a condemnation of being
blatantly antigay. The world has dramatically shifted.

Elders say, "How easy it is to forget." Young ones
say, "Get out of the way and stop living in the past."

. . .

Times change. Issues evolve. History proves that we
learn our lessons best when we remember how we got

to where we are. It also proves that we grow best when we allow the young to continue building the roads according to their own vision. We can only hope that we will each have the vision and courage to learn what has come before and be activated in a way that guides the future.

We, of Generation Queer, have more in common than our various ages would at first reveal. We are the queers who happen to be homosexual. That is our common ground. We don't get to function from easy assumptions; we must earn our way to paradise. When we truly realize just how much we have to teach each other, our road building goes faster. The key to our greatest future, to the future where we can all just get on with our lives, is to turn toward each other and learn, to bring our perspectives together and grow.

4

THE CROSS ROOM

Infinite Spirit,
Help me to see clearly when my heart turns
hard. Help me to look for hope and not for hope-
lessness. Help me to live my life with truth. Help
me to live my ideal life, not as a destroyer, but as
a contributor to building peace in this world.
Help me to see that the changes I seek must first
come about within me; that if I want the world to
change, I must start at home. Help me seek divine
truth. I ask for a miracle of change. Help me to
see through the eyes of love. Thank you. Amen.

■ ■ ■

It felt as if I had fallen into a trap. A few years ago, the
shifting foundations of my life led me to wonder if

every belief I'd ever had had been changed overnight. I began to slip, to fall; I tried to hold myself up, but slipped into some self-destructive behaviors. I started drinking more than I had in my entire adult life. I had begun to lose control. I couldn't help questioning everything. How could I have been so wrong? I wondered. It felt as if I had painted myself into a corner. I had challenged too many boundaries, in myself and in the world around me, and now it was time to pay the price.

One of my extremely bigoted relatives had predicted—right after I'd come out in the media in the late '80s—that I had ruined my life and that I'd thrown away all hope for any success. At the time I told him to go screw himself, but wondered if, in fact, he might not be right. For several years it seemed as if his prediction had been miles off the mark, but then everything in my life felt as if it had changed. I questioned everything before finally settling down to the inner work that seemed to be presenting itself.

Feeling trapped by my own life I began to wonder, asking God—more peevishly than prayerfully—why I had been given such a heavy burden. I'd begun to feel as if all my life, I'd been the outsider, the underdog, underestimated and misjudged at every turn. I'd always been so queer. The pain felt overwhelming. I'd let myself slide, because I felt as if everything I'd done had been for nothing—all the activism, the career sidetracks, the exhaustion, the exhilaration—for nothing. How would I ever turn this around? I asked myself. I had begun to feel all those same things I'd felt when I was eighteen years old and just beginning to fully deal with being queer. I felt lost.

■ ■ ■

I knew that I needed to turn it around. There was no way on earth I was going to stay lost. I had been so worried about what others would think—all the pestering critics of how my activism had come about—that I'd gotten sidetracked from exploring what I thought. What were my beliefs about change? I began to look into my heart, to realize that I had frozen my pain in thick ice, that I had been holding it at bay, wishing it would go away, for years. Now I had the opportunity to really face it and shrink it—to look the pain straight in the eyes and tell it that I wasn't going to give in.

I began to walk the woods and beaches of my new island home, hoping that such a natural, unspoiled, isolated location would hold some answers. It did, but not quite the answers I had anticipated.

It came to me one day while I was wading around a tide pool, carefully examining the tiny creatures who lived there in their own little universe. It was a day that was richly cloudy; rain had been coming in slanted needles all morning, yet I was out in it and happy. I was going to have to catch a ferry to America so that I could travel a couple of thousand miles to give a lecture the next evening. I had determined months earlier that it was all the travel, all the hundreds of lectures in different cities, all the turmoil of being away from home so much that contributed to the shift in my life—the loss of direction and hope. I had decided, because of that, to rarely travel again, but here I was starting to lecture again. And I was happy.

I knew that I could leave home now and not lose my center. I had thought that if I put myself in a location I deemed spiritual to my own nature, I could achieve some sort of enlightenment more quickly. What I started to discover instead was that holiness wasn't dependent on a location, but on me—where I was inside my own head and heart. The outside could be a paradise or a prison, depending on how I saw it. I was not a victim of some circumstance; I was its co-creator. We all are. Each of us co-creates this world and then interprets our own creation and the creation of others according to how we want to see things. There were certainly times when living in what I thought was paradise felt like being in a prison cell, just as there were other times when being in some place that wasn't home could feel right and good.

. . .

Whenever I begin to feel sorry for myself, whenever the world feels as if it has given me an unbearable burden, I remember something a dear friend gave me to read. A few years ago, he saw that my life appeared in shambles, mainly because I wasn't hiding where I was—psychologically, emotionally, spiritually—from those I was close to. Instinctively I knew enough to reach out and take the chance that I could be vulnerable with my closest friends.

This friend had been listening to me talk about my perceived burdens for about a half an hour. He listened patiently until I got to the point where I was beginning to paint my burden—my pain—as somehow greater than anyone could ever understand. He asked me to hang on a second, crossed the living room and went into a cupboard, from which he pulled out a piece of worn paper. "Here, read this," he had said, handing it to me. He told me that his grandma had given it to him when he'd told her that he was gay. She had been so understanding, but drew the line when he had begun going on too long about how hard his life was, feeling way too sorry for himself. I looked at the paper. It was a story I'd known from boyhood, from Sunday school, but had forgotten. There was no attribution, no name of the original author on the paper, but it went something like this:

A young man was at the end of his rope. Seeing no way out, he dropped to his knees and prayed. "Dear God, I can't go on. The cross I have to bear is too big and heavy."

God replied, "My son, I love you and do not want to see you suffer. If you can't bear the weight of your cross then place it inside this room. Then open that door over there, go inside and pick out any cross you wish."

The young man was filled with relief and sighed, "Thank you, God." When he entered the room through the door, as God had instructed, he saw thousands of crosses. Some were so large that the tops stretched up out of sight. After looking around amazed, he spotted a tiny cross leaning against a far wall.

"Please, God, I'll take that one," he said.

And God replied, "My son, that is the cross you just brought in."

I read that and was reminded that I can feel sorry for myself, but that only ensures that I will be immobilized, that I will stand in the way of my own growth. Do I experience oppression and heartache as a queer? Yes. However, it is up to me whether or not I give it any weight, whether or not I see my life as gifted or cursed. I had experienced a divorce—something that millions of other people go through—and began questioning everything about my existence. I was giving in to the sad belief that I had no right to be human, to experience setbacks, to make errors, to cry, because I was queer and had to prove something more, live up to a higher standard than straight people.

At that point, all the evidence in my life said that in spite of a setback, things were still great and could get better. At last, I could let myself feel pain, without indulging in the pain as the core of my identity. I had watched too many friends and acquaintances get caught in the trap of nurturing their pain like a favorite pet bird, kept in the warmest spot in the house and claimed as a full identity. Their pain was straw pride, faux wisdom. It is easy to think this way. There are so many images in queer culture that seem to battle back and forth between the eternal circuit party and crushing oppression, never fully examining how deeply they are attached. No matter how far we come as a culture, we still struggle against the weight of the myths and lies; sometimes we polish up the lousy ideas we have about ourselves, as if they are awards and not traps. If you don't believe that just go into any gay disco and watch the amount of drugs and alcohol consumed—not just consumed to the point of stupor, but worshipped as if the consumption was a demonstration of enlightenment and not nihilism.

. . .

As a community we must stop arguing for our fragility, for the prisons of our self-limitations. We must look beneath the surface and truly examine—in ourselves—what still disgusts us. When do we truly see that it all rests in our hands? Our burdens may be great, but they are only the biggest and heaviest if we refuse to look around and see how many others have greater burdens than we do.

We must go to the heart of our love/hate relationships with our queer selves. Don't call self-destructive behavior self-love. Don't think that being an activist, or having an active sex life, automatically makes you self-loving. For most of us the rotten ideas we have about ourselves don't necessarily present themselves on the surface; they run deep. Have the courage to look and be honest. We were given our crosses in life so that we can learn, so that our souls can grow. I believe that with every fiber of my being.

. . .

My own growth had felt stalled and it took a bolt of honestly embraced lightning to get me back on track, to make me realize that perhaps my growth—as both a man and as a queer—had been on the right course all along.

I've often wondered how much of the myths and lies I was raised with still cling to the deepest part of me. How many of us do all this work, even becoming activists, but still way deep down believe ourselves to be perverts? How much of our community's ongoing struggle with nihilism and our tendency to eat our own grows out of clinging to the last remnants of lies? There are no general answers, but to go forward, I must be willing to look for the answers to these issues in my own heart and I must encourage others to do the same—with absolute, unflinching honesty.

We must break the cycle that has bigots pointing to the self-destruction in our community, saying, "See, I told you they were screwed up." Instead, we must acknowledge that our nihilism stems from lies. The anti-gay bigot has it wrong. The nihilism isn't the source, it's the result of a system that, even though it is slowly changing, still tells lies about queers. It is time for us to stand up and call lies lies, and we should be doing this each in our own unique way. Some will take to the streets, others will go about it quietly. Neither method is superior, they are simply different.

. . .

I was having dinner with two gay men one night. I didn't know either of them all that well. We'd been acquainted for a few months; I was trying to reach out and make new friends, so I decided to be completely honest and bring up the ideas I'd been having about still fighting against self-hate. Although it was subtle, I still had moments when I held being queer against myself and there were fleeting times when I thought it represented the biggest burden imaginable. I told them that it was anything but blatant, yet it was definitely where the rest of my own struggle lay, and that I'd only really decided it was going on after I'd undertaken a brutally honest search of my own heart.

At first they both expressed shock. They knew me as someone who was an activist and who seemed completely self-accepting. I tried to reinforce that I was talking about subtle currents, feelings that I'd really had to dig hard to find, to name. Then I asked them both to be honest and tell me if they'd ever felt the same things, if they ever held being queer against themselves. They both vehemently denied being in the least self-hating, and both expressed surprise that I was. I tried again to explain, but couldn't seem to get through what I was saying. They both saw themselves—at least for our conversation—as being at the end of the trail. What revealed itself through the course of that evening, though, both confused and enlightened me.

Later, at the end of dinner, one man said that he'd never come out to his family and had no intention of ever doing so, but offered no further explanation; he grew visibly uncomfortable at this line of conversation. The other said that his relationship with his family was very bad and had gotten worse since he'd come out to them. Both had earlier revealed—in roundabout ways—that neither of them was really out at work. After dinner we went to a dance club and for the next five hours I watched my new friends do nearly every drug imaginable, drink vodka until staggeringly drunk, and blindly twirl the night away. The next day I learned that this was pretty much a weekly ritual for them, every week from Thursday until Sunday.

. . .

We do not need to be a generation lost in cynicism, fear, and unquenchable anger. If we, as queers, truly want our peaceful place in this world, we must find our balance. Is it fair that we seem to be held to higher standards than others? Perhaps not. But we are not the first group of people to fight for respect against a cold riptide of lies. It may seem that fate has dealt us a terrible hand (even if we refuse to admit that we feel this way sometimes), but if we are honest, if we truly go into the heart of the matter, the hand we have been given is not a curse but a gift. It is a gift which can help us become extraordinary. Do not turn away. Do not hide. Listen to your own highest voice—the voice of God—tell you that you are loved and that you deserve that love. That's not feel-good, New-Agey nonsense. It's the truth. Don't let the cynics convince you otherwise.

. . .

We each come into this world with guiding spirits, elements of energy that guide the course of our lives. For each of us there is a life path that, when followed, reveals our true calling. In many cases finding that true calling, when the deck seems so stacked against us in so many ways, becomes a lifesaver. By healing our hearts and turning our attention toward finding our highest path, we open our lives to the possibility of fulfillment beyond our wildest expectations. We have been beaten down and pushed around long enough. We must begin to see that we change the world when we change ourselves. We change ourselves when we are true to our own individual hearts and callings.

· · ·

I must ask myself if I expect less from my life because I am queer. I must especially ask myself this during times when, on the gift-curse continuum, I feel the curse is like a monster breathing, hot and putrid, at my shoulder. I must look deep within myself and find the source, turn around and face the monster's steaming breath, while simultaneously avoiding becoming so engrossed in looking at the monster that I miss out on life. So how do I look inside my own heart at the wounds when it feels far easier to distract myself from them, to pretend they're not there, to lash out at others to cover up my own pain? How can I reclaim my wholeness, and work toward remembering my own divinity, as one small part of God, when it feels as if the crest of every hill hides another battle?

. . .

I believe with all my soul that I was put on this earth for a reason. I believe that we all were. None of our reasons are superior to anyone else's. It seems so easy, even when delving into the spiritual, to resort to some natural competitiveness, a sort of "I'm more enlightened than you are" smugness. That superiority complex is what is at the root of the bigotry I fight against, so how can I do anything except reject it? If the root equation is what I believe it to be—that to get love, we must be loving—then the equivalent here is surely that if we do not want to be seen as spiritually inferior, we must reject our own urges to claim a spiritual superiority over others.

What I need to answer for myself is this: where does this anger come from, this madness that lies right beneath the surface, that feels as if it permeates every part of me and is ready to boil like some wild river? In every conversation that even mildly touches on queer rights I feel this thing rise up. I feel some sense of anger at any queer who isn't doing everything possible to change the world. Try as I might not to, I end up thinking that people who aren't fighting for their rights just steal the fruit and then carve their initials in the tree trunk, and take the efforts of others for granted.

Where does this barely bridled rage come from, this tornado that builds in my stomach every time I speak of queer issues, even in the midst of a seemingly peaceful, spiritual conversation? I can feel its swirling wind begin to rise whenever I hear someone tell me that radical activism is the wrong path, that I'm too radical, or that I'm not radical enough.

What is that thing in my heart that responds so automatically whenever I see one of those little Christian fish symbols on the back of a car? How do I simultaneously fight for my rights and reject seeing every fundamentalist Christian as a hypocritical bigot?

The other day, I was driving along a freeway and passed a car with personalized license plates that said something obviously intended to identify the driver as a hardcore Christian, and there was one of those little chrome fish symbols right there on the edge of the trunk. I automatically began drawing conclusions about everyone in the car—they were this, they were that, and most especially they had to be antigay, mean-spirited hypocrites. I shocked myself. Here I thought that I'd done all this work on becoming a loving man, one who tried not to hold harsh judgments about anyone, and I was triggered to severe judgment by a license plate and bumper decoration. I had slipped into the same mindset that seems to fight for free speech and thought so long as it's thought and speech that I agree with. I slipped into the same mindset that I'd always criticized in others.

How were my judgments any different than the ones some people automatically made about me, or other queers? Wasn't I just participating in the same thing? I know that some activists would try to rationalize away that equivalence, but I can't. If I expect love, I must be loving. If I demand respect for my differences, I must respect the differences of others.

■ ■ ■

Humans tend to develop hierarchies of discrimination, of oppression, as if there is only so much freedom to go around. It happens inside communities—one faction screaming at another—and between different communities. No matter where it happens, it is a limiting perspective, this screaming out: my people were more oppressed than your people, we have been held down for longer, or, you are self-hating because you're (fill in the blank). Rants of this kind are arguments for limitation. They ignore the possibilities of unlimited love—of the boundless power that we each hold, of our ability to define our own lives in either positive or negative directions. They say that the world blows us along its course and we are helpless against the tide, that we are small and limited and weak.

How can we argue for the limitations of our spirits? Does it really serve the cause of justice to scream out to the world that your people have suffered longer than another's and therefore the other's needs should be ignored while yours are addressed? Wouldn't it be far more fair to say that as long as there is any injustice, any oppression left in the world, our journey toward freedom continues?

It seems that in every struggle, so much energy is spent on division, on putting down those who see things differently, that the path can be obscured as if lost in a heavy fog of fear. Differences are not the enemy. We cannot say to the world that we celebrate our diversity and then call each other nasty names.

In the queer community labels get thrown around all the time that are intended to wound. They aren't always labels that would be considered all that negative in the mainstream world, but when you're an outsider, you know which otherwise innocuous terms are meant to hurt.

. . .

There's an old saying that's heard so often inside the queer community, especially among activists, that it has become a cliché: We eat our own.

There's more truth in that statement than most of us want to admit. For some, slashing the figurative jugular veins of other queer brothers and sisters has become such a gleefully perfected sport that we probably have our true enemies lining up to get front-row tickets on the fifty-yard line of this world-championship-level game of gay nihilism. Men against women, conservative against liberal, urban against rural, young against old, and on and on. So many divisions, so much unnecessary infighting.

To continue on a forward course, our nihilism must end and it should have stopped yesterday. If only we would all stop for a while to really figure out where this particular form of destruction comes from; if only we'd stop giving lip service and really—once and for all—look at it, really search for its roots, not in each other—the place where usual human instincts assign all blame—but in ourselves; if only we would actually take the most dramatic leap a human soul can take:

the leap toward absolute honesty and personal responsibility. If only.

. . .

When we eat our own it is because our hearts are not
healed and because at some level we still believe all the
lies and myths. We eat our own because to destroy those
like us is to destroy the part of ourselves we despise. Self-
hatred rests among the deepest of cardinal sins. It is
here, in addressing our divisions, which so many times
are but vapors of illusion, that our greatest struggle may
rest. It is here that so many find confusion. In this struggle, those who seek self-aggrandizement rather than justice abuse the natural human tendency to succumb to
tribalisms and division. We must reject the divisive messages of those who seek their own selfish advancement
through this movement. This struggle is not about indi-
viduals building personal political empires, it is about
the individual struggle toward self-respect.

Beware the prophets of false division. Beware
those who wish to keep us divided against each other,
those who exploit our wounds in order to hold off their
own obsolescence. It is vital that we look at the history
of other movements similar to ours. There are lessons
there. When measuring leaders and their priorities,
look to see who tries to divide and who attempts to

unite. Who among us seeks their own power at the expense of others? Who exploits our remaining wounds? We must swim—with all our might—against the riptide of superficial labels and petty accusations to find our Heaven on earth.

. . .

I live on an island now. It is a home that resonates with my truest soul, not only because the woods and beaches make my heart sing, but because of what it represents to me. It is a place both connected and separate. I am in America, yet apart. It is a reflection of my life, of my deepest spiritual choir, a place of solos and million-part harmonies. I have found my home.

That is also how I feel about my ongoing struggle with this thing that twines around so many of my emotions, this queer thing that has come to the center of my life. It occupies so much space in my interior life, yet it is a vapor. I wish so much for it to become a nothing issue to me, but know that I haven't yet earned that right; that to give in now—to look, see, yet walk away—would be to deny this piece of my soul's struggle against the entropic forces of life's great gravity. It winds around me, comes up over me, takes my breath away when I realize that I am kissing a man good morning, brings me joy, catches—every so often—in my throat, helps make me whole. This queer thing has brought me a gift beyond the magic of great romantic love. It has brought into my life the catalyst for creating tremendous self-love; it has given me the strength to push a thousand of life's boulders across the starkest of valleys, build magnificent walls, and create temples of celebration. This gift, enfolded as it can be in curse's bleak wrapping, has spawned in me the eyes to look at someone—the other—whom I might otherwise turn my back on and realize that he or she is my sister or brother. Children of God, Goddess, Infinite Spirit, we come together. Difference means nothing. We are dancing spirits living on a rock in the middle of the ocean, passing the time, watching a sunset. And our lives grow more magnificent each day.

> *Dear God,*
> *Help me to see and understand the struggle of others. Help me to remember that I am not alone on this journey toward Your love. Open my eyes. Open my heart. Help me to see and understand that I cannot build my spirit by hurting others. Allow me to love those who condemn me. Help me, God. I need Your strength to fill me so that I may be a part of the planet's healing. Help me to find heart. Amen.*

PART
TWO

A QUEER NUMBER OF
QUESTIONS AND ANSWERS

During the past several years I have traveled around the country—giving college lectures, attending and organizing fund-raisers, meeting with community groups and national leaders—and have learned under fire just how much there is to feel optimistic about in the queer rights movement. I have witnessed, at picnics and parades, youth meetings and funerals, the broad palette of our community. It has been inspiring to see the actual diversity of our queer community: in lives lived in the cities, out in the suburbs, and on the farms; lives spent deeply closeted and proudly open; from in-your-face activists, pushing the horizons of what is possible, to families that come to embrace a gay child as an equal, important part of that family's fabric.

It has been an amazing, exhausting journey, a roller coaster of encounter and experience. Throughout the entire process, even when my exhausted mind screamed out to just put everything on autopilot, I tried to keep my eyes, mind, and heart open to differences of opinion and to criticisms that sometimes shredded my spirit. I can honestly say that I grew into a full, mature, out-all-the-time-no-matter-what, socially responsible queer man. Out on the road, I grew up.

In the first part of this book I tried to openly share some of my observations and opinions about queer life. I am the first to admit that everything in the previous chapters revolves around my own biased opinions. However, it's my hope that I have expressed my observations and ideas with compassion. I especially hope that I have sparked ideas in you, and that you will be encouraged to participate, or continue participating, in queer rights issues, and will do so with a loving and open heart.

I now want to share with you a variety of letters that have come in to me over the last few years. Because a lot of my activism was in the public eye, I have had tens of thousands of people write to me in the years since I first came out in the media. The letters have come from all over the nation and the world and have covered every conceivable aspect of queer life. I have selected letters that represent a wide variety of issues and perspectives, and have edited these letters in such a way that the privacy of the person writing has been maintained. I have done my best to answer their questions with compassion and honesty. I am offering opinions here. I make no claim that I have the only, or final, answer. The answers I give are the result of my own experience and evolution. They come from my heart.

When I address these issues, I do so realizing that we all have different life experiences, different expectations and desires. While we may not see our exact lives reflected in each question and answer, there can be deeper meanings for us in examining the soulful struggle of others. In other words, please don't assume that just because a particular section doesn't seem to apply to you that you should just pass it by. I would ask only that, as I have attempted to answer each question with heart, you also open your own heart. We sometimes learn the strongest lessons of our lives through observing the process of others.

When we look at the world with love—with an open heart—we never know what wondrous thing will present itself.

QUESTION I: I am a thirty-four-year-old straight woman living in North Dakota. As a high school teacher for the past six years, I've worked with all sorts of young men and women. I'm writing to you for advice about a situation I am currently dealing with. One of my students has recently been showing signs of extreme stress (falling grades, losing weight, fatigue, cutting class, etc.). I hear him being teased a great deal by fellow students about how everyone knows he is gay. Personally, I suspect that he is gay and on more than one occasion he has approached me with a "there's something I need to talk with you about," but as yet hasn't allowed himself to open up. I am concerned about him. He's extremely bright and shows great potential. I see how relentless teenagers can be with their teasing.

The reason I chose to write to you is because my younger brother, who is gay, saw you when you spoke at his college several years ago. Your words helped him tremendously as he struggled with his own coming out. I want to help my student. What words of advice do you have for me and other concerned teachers who see young men and women struggling with this issue?

ANSWER 1: Your question is among the most difficult I have ever faced. You would be surprised at how many educators are in a situation similar to yours. By saying that, I do not mean to diminish the seriousness of what you and your student face, but mean only that this is a timely and broad-based issue. I'll try to answer your question in both a larger, more global way and a more local, specific way.

First, very encouraging news, which reflects directly upon you: in the broadest sense, it is a tremendous leap forward that a teacher would want to deal with this issue in a positive way with a student. That certainly is a change from twenty years ago when I was in high school and just beginning to deal with my queerness. I didn't think that I had anywhere to turn and saw absolutely no positive images in the media, or anywhere else, that reflected any hint about gay life. I felt absolutely alone and helpless. I don't think that any of my teachers would have looked at the signs you are seeing in your student—including the taunting by other students—and read them as a signal that positive support was needed. My sense always was that teachers thought that the teasing might just get the student to make the "right choice" and somehow decide that he was straight after all—as if the negative peer pressure would convince a wayward tribe member to wise up and conform to the group.

Perhaps we are slowly breaking past the myth that someone can be persuaded toward homosexuality, and that with just the right influence can be persuaded to be straight instead. It has been said so many times by so many gay people, but it bears repeating, because old myths break down by replacing them over and over again with the truth. It goes back to what I've said in lecture after lecture when dealing with issues of the development of queer sexuality. If you want to know about gay people ask a gay person. Don't turn to some straight fundamentalist preacher, or some right-wing, fear-mongering politician, to understand gays. Go to the horses' mouths. An overwhelming majority of queers know for a fact that they did not choose to be gay. I still can't understand why that is so difficult for some people to understand, but it is. Queer sexuality develops just like non-queer sexuality does. Our culture continues to make way too much of an issue out of developments that are remarkably similar, except for some minor details.

That directly ties in to how this student's taunters are treating him. Your students are at an age when sexuality is bubbling up at a frenzied pace and issues around conformity and group and individual identity are being battled out, as teenagers prepare themselves to go into the world and make their way. The gay person still represents the acceptable target for energies directed against those who are different from the dominant culture. So your mission is figuring out a strategy for how to reach this young man—and others like him who might pass through your classroom—in a positive way.

There are a few questions you should answer for your own clarity. First, what is it that you want to accomplish here? I would imagine that you want to assure this student a better quality of life, to assure that he makes it through the hell of living through high school as an outsider. I would imagine that your brother probably told you how rough he had it growing up gay and you want to make sure that no kid under your guidance has to go through that. I'm only guessing of course, but I know that's what I feel when I do gay youth fund-raising, when I try to decide where to best direct my efforts. If those are also your instincts, then my sense is that you are on the right path. Specifics, though, you need some specifics.

That leads to the next question you should ask yourself: What is your current relationship with this student? Your actions must target his individuality. Have you had many previous interactions from which you can draw instruction? For example, have you ever, even gently, pushed an issue with him? You say that he has approached you tentatively, letting you know that there is something he needs to talk about. That is a major opening. He's probably waiting for your move. I would have been. Having cracked the door, even a little, on this issue, I would have been scared to death to push further, no matter how open the teacher was. It sounds as if the ball has been placed squarely in your court.

A couple of other questions to ask yourself: Do you know of any existing support systems in your community? Are there any other staff at your school or in your system who might be a positive ally on this issue (a counselor, for example)? Now, an important part of answering that last question is the understanding that another teacher that you suppose, or even know, to be gay, may or may not be a good choice of an ally to turn to. If a teacher is in any way closeted, he or she might react in a negative way to your request for any help. You might also be surprised to know how many older gays think that queer kids should just have to tough it out, because that's what they had to do. This is probably just a mask, though, to avoid getting caught up in an issue that could raise traumatic issues for a gay (especially a closeted gay) educator.

Do you know this young man's parents? What are their general world views? I'm asking this only so that you can have a sense of what the student's home life must be like, not as a suggestion that you bring the parents in. That could well get him thrown out in the street, or on the other hand could help create a strong support system, but it's hard to tell from the outside.

How has your brother dealt with his homosexuality? Would you consider him to be well-adjusted and happy? Ask him. Tell him about your situation and ask him what he would have wanted you to do. Ask him if he minds if you talk about his gayness in any conversations you might have with your student. You may have already resolved this issue within your family, but in many families it hasn't been established where the boundaries of openness lie.

Now after considering all of these issues, I would ask you to spend some time quietly turning your heart over to your highest guidance. Find the clearest voice for your instinct. Write down what you want to accomplish from your actions, to clarify where you're headed. Now schedule a time when you can speak with your student in absolute privacy. Assure him that—unless you get his permission or feel as if his life is in danger—you will keep everything you two discuss in absolute confidence. Issue number one in your conversation with him is to help him see that what he is going through is normal. I cannot stress this enough. After you have confirmed that he is indeed struggling with his sexuality, normalize, normalize, normalize. Be sympathetic. Also do your homework ahead of your

meeting. Be prepared for the possibility that your conversation might scare him off for a while. Come in
with pamphlets or books and other resources; give
them to him as soon as the opportunity presents itself,
just in case he bolts mid-conversation. Call your local
chapter of PFLAG (Parents and Friends of Lesbians
and Gays) for assistance with local resources. They
should be listed in the phone book. If not, try their
main office in Washington, D.C. PFLAG's main goal
is to normalize gay issues for families. They are a
wealth of information for what you are going through.
Have them send you information. I would also suggest
finding a gay youth support group or professional
counselor in your area; the counselor may be necessary if the student continues on the self-destructive
path you describe. Your goal with your student should
be to make his integration of his sexuality a positive experience. Suggest to him that he develop a pen pal relationship with another kid in similar circumstances
(gay youth groups can be helpful with this).

The taunting by other students is a sticky situation. While your school system may have some form of
protection for students who are being harassed, using
that protection might make the situation worse, by
drawing attention to the student. Perhaps in this case,
as an initial step, more emphasis should be placed on

helping the student grow stronger, so that the taunts mean less. However, I do want to stress that if the harassment is, or becomes, so severe that no other course of action will help, you should not hesitate to go to your superiors to seek action. This student has the right to get his education without harassment for who he is. School authorities should be made aware—if things get to that point—that they could be held liable should they know about blatant, discriminatory harassment and do nothing about it.

Whatever route presents itself, use your inner guidance. You are doing God's work. You could well be helping to save this student's life. You are to be praised for that. I am praying for the highest resolution of your circumstances and other situations like it.

QUESTION 2: I came out to my mother over three years ago when I was sixteen. She was cool about it but made me swear that I wouldn't tell my father, who she claims will flip out and probably throw me out of the house. At first it didn't bother me; I was able to tell my mother pretty much everything I wanted to and she was fine with my being gay. We grew to be very close. Closer than I imagine that we would have been if I had remained in the closet. The problem is that my relationship with my father has suffered a lot. I'm at the point where I hate lying to him and want so badly to tell him I am gay. But my mother is right when she tells me that he just isn't as accepting as she is. And he has a horrible temper. My mother keeps warning me (probably accurately) that he'll stop paying my college tuition if he finds out that I am queer. I've only got a year left before I graduate. Do I wait to tell him and finish school and just ignore the responsibility that I have to myself? Or do I tell him and risk screwing up my education and maybe even being thrown out of the house?

ANSWER 2: A year left until graduation, huh? The easy and I suppose hardcore activist thing for me to say would be that you should ignore all circumstances to the contrary and come out to your dad; damn the consequences. Oh, if the world were so perfect. But, if it were, I suppose that there wouldn't be any need to come out to Dad at all. Sadly, that just isn't the world that we live in—yet. Our mission is to make sure that, with all of our efforts, we continuously nudge our own individual worlds closer to that ideal.

I see a lot of positive effort in what you tell me. First of all you were able to self-identify at a fairly young age. It sounds as if you created a positive experience for yourself in doing so, too. Within a short time you came out to some family, which for many queers is the most frightening experience imaginable. You successfully conquered that fear, and are to be commended for that. I don't think that our community says enough good things to each other, such as congratulating each other for leaping over significant hurdles. Also look at what you demonstrated to yourself: you came out to your mom and have built a positive, close relationship with her. I'm sure that didn't happen by accident. It took effort on both your parts. All those things are very positive. I would encourage you to take a few moments—not only now, but on a regular, ongoing basis—to be grateful for those positives.

The other positives I see in the life you describe are that you have continued your education and don't want to do anything to jeopardize graduating from college. You are obviously responsible and mature. Given that you have this perspective, I'd like for you to consider a few things, which may assist you in your decision regarding your dad. On what is your mom's advice, to not come out to Dad, based? Ask her. Has she actually heard him say the words? Did you have a gay sibling (or someone else in or close to the family) who got an angry reaction from Dad? Has he expressed antigay sentiments in the past? It's in variables such as these that you will be able to truly determine your correct course of action.

Now, let's assume for the moment that your fears are true. If you came out to Dad he would react badly and not only cut off school funding, but also kick you out of the house. If, after examining all the other factors in a rational manner, you guessed that this would be the case, my advice—in direct opposition to my "perfect world" advice—would be to delay coming out to Dad until after graduation. In a sense, your dad has indicated that it is his responsibility to pay for your education. It is an education that you deserve and one that will give you an advantage out in the real world. And let's face it, one of the best means of quality revenge against the bigotry queers face is achieving successes in our lives—not just financially, but in happiness, fulfillment, and spiritual values. So do whatever you can to get through until graduation.

The other side of the above advice would be to examine your fears and the fears of your mom more closely. Is your mom's fear based on issues she still has with your being gay? Is she projecting those feelings onto Dad? Are you creating more fear than is merited? Would Dad really react in such a strident, negative way? Would he actually undermine his son's future on a whim? If, after analyzing these things, you determine that it is worth risking the unpredictability of Dad's reaction, then plan the most positive coming out imaginable. Work through it with your mom and any other supportive family members. Have reading material on gay issues available for Dad (contact PFLAG, or a gay friendly bookstore for these types of materials). Pray, meditate, clear your mind—whatever it takes for you to center your energies—before sitting down with Dad, if you should decide that the time is now. Do it with love. Above all else, please remember—and it is easy, given the negative images we sometimes deal with—that, no matter when you come out to your dad, what you are telling him is positive information. There is nothing negative at all about your being queer. Nothing. However you decide to handle the situation, I hope that it brings your family closer together.

QUESTION 3: I am writing this letter out of desperation. Until about a month ago my life was perfect. I met a great man about six months ago. He isn't my first gay relationship but this is definitely my first serious one. I'm twenty-six and came out to myself when I was twenty-one but I have not come out to my parents or sister yet. I intend to but I am just not ready yet. The problem is my boyfriend. He began putting pressure on me to come out to my family recently. He is very open with his family and has been since he was seventeen. I respect that, but we are definitely moving at a different pace when it comes to this. I'm not ready yet. But, as I feared, the ultimatum was handed down last week— tell my family or we break up until I come out. I love my boyfriend and am horrified at the thought of losing him. But I don't feel I can do this now. My life has gone from heaven to hell in a matter of weeks and I don't know what to do. How can I handle this?

ANSWER 3: It is obvious that you are experiencing a great deal of pain. Your question cuts right to the heart of what is so difficult about being queer. We aren't allowed to take for granted what non-gays do. Things such as relationships, romances, heartbreaks, and the other ups and downs of life become magnified by how open or closed our lives are.

You raise several issues, but your main question revolves around your boyfriend, so let me address that first. Your boyfriend has now given you a come-out-or-get-dumped ultimatum. And herein lies one of the key issues in the development of strong gay identities. Some of us view coming out as the ultimate necessity, others don't. We cannot take each of our different levels of comfort and create a hierarchy. Your boyfriend was obviously comfortable coming out to his family at a younger age. Does that make him superior to you on some arbitrary queer scale? I don't think so. To automatically say that he is superior because of his family status is to ignore how tightly our identities intertwine with our family ties. And in a perfect world, no coming out would be necessary. Coming out at all only exists because of a history of prejudice.

You guys both probably need to take a breath. Sit your boyfriend down for a strong heart to heart. He needs to learn some patience. You've been together six months. An ultimatum at this stage (or any stage, for that matter) of a relationship seems like more of a power and control struggle than anything else. Should he hope that you are as out as he is? Sure. But his ultimatum smacks of emotional blackmail, of my-way-or-the-highway thinking. If he loves you and is in this for the long haul, he should be helping you in a compassionate way. This business of "do it my way or get dumped" is abusive—period—especially given the difficulty of this issue. You guys should give strong consideration to getting some professional counseling so that you can sit down and really get into this matter in a loving way. If your boyfriend refuses to consider counseling, or says that it's your problem and not his—that you're the one who needs help, not him—then you might have a more serious problem. You might consider whether or not he will continue using these serious control issues.

However, it does appear—especially as you speak of your love for him, which I assume is equally reciprocated—as if there is a good possibility for a positive resolution here, one through which you both can get your needs met. But it's going to take that greatest of relationship skills—the one that can make or break even the most passionate of loves—and that is compassionate compromise. He is going to need to explore why he so needs to control you and you will need to explore why you are allowing yourself to be worked. And, by the way, these issues present themselves in many relationships. You guys aren't alone.

Now I want to address the secondary issues raised in your letter. Are you happy with the way your life is structured? As you are living it now, you must exclude so much information when talking with family. The exchange of information is—because of the secret in your life—so uneven, it is not truly fair to you or those you remain closeted to. Are you—in your heart of hearts—happy with that?

In your question, you say that you aren't ready to come out to your family right now. I'd like for you to think about the time when you are ready. Visualize this. Picture in your mind that you are at a time when all your family knows you for who you are. Not only that, but you're at a time when you've worked through the entire coming out process with them and integrated your boyfriend into your family interactions. Can you picture this? What had to happen in order for you to get from where you are now to where you are in that visualization of the future? What actual, real-world steps did you take to get yourself there? It's important to stress here that I really mean, what steps did you take? You are the only one who has total responsibility here. This rests on your perceptions.

Now, before you start thinking that I'm being too hard-assed, I want to say that I sympathize with your position. My guess is that you fear that coming out would be more painful than the pain you are experiencing closeted. Oh, except that you say that your life was perfect until your boyfriend made his ultimatum. But let me ask you this, in the most loving, compassionate way possible: How perfect has your life really been in the five years since you came out to yourself and right now? Does your view of perfection include having a chasm between yourself and your family?

Again, I don't ask these things in judgment, but to get you to think about where your life is. The important thing is to not beat yourself up for things you wish you'd done differently, or ignore those things that need your attention. How can you get on the path, or speed up the process toward getting comfortable with coming out to your family? What needs to change? Or more accurately, what about your world view needs to change so that you can get through this frightening process successfully? That, beyond anything else, is the core concern.

My strongest suggestion to you is to get yourself on the path toward coming out to your family. Get a sympathetic and compassionate counselor. Read some books. Join a group. Do whatever it takes to get on the road, but do it because you want to, not because of pressure from your boyfriend.

QUESTION 4: I am a forty-three-year-old divorced woman and am writing to you for some much needed advice. I was married for almost twenty years and the fact that it ended is a good thing. That definitely isn't the problem.

After my divorce I returned to school and met a man who has become my absolute best friend. He's thirty-two and gay. I've known all along and it was never a problem. Actually it has really enlightened me as a person. The problem is that I love this man. He is kind and sweet and the most intelligent and attractive man I've ever known. I've heard that it is common for straight women to fall for their gay male best friends. Is this true? I have dated men during our friendship and will continue to do so. But they consistently turn out to be such jerks. Most are so emotionally unavailable and haven't got an idea about how to talk to a woman or what we really want. Yet my friend is always right on the target with all of that. Why am I so convinced that I will never find a straight man with such wonderful qualities?

My real concern, and consequently my question to you, is can I remain friends with this man when I feel the way that I do? Should I tell him? I am afraid to jeopardize our very special friendship. What is the best way to handle this?

ANSWER 4: My initial answer to your question is that, yes, you can remain friends with this man. Your situation is so common that entire books have been written about the relationship between straight women and gay men. For many women who have gay male friends, the friendship might well represent the first, or deepest, nonromantic adult male/female friendship in both people's lives. That the friendship, where two people connect so well, doesn't automatically evolve into romance can be confusing, especially for you as a non-gay person. As simplistic as it may sound for someone romantically and physically attracted to the opposite sex, romance remains something of a possibility in a friendship with a man. Your friend isn't—as a rule—romantically attracted to you as a woman, so the possibility of anything beyond friendship probably doesn't enter his mind. From his perspective, your situation would be as if he had an extremely close friendship with a non-gay man and fell in love with him; possibilities of any real romance would be slim to none.

You will need to go deep inside your heart and realize that what you wish would happen, in all probability, will not take place. You must set out to create a dramatic shift. However, this is going to take some effort on your part. Unless he has given you clear signals otherwise (and you don't indicate that he has), your friend is not responsible for your romantic feelings toward him. It sounds as if he is simply being himself. As difficult as it may be, you will need to do a couple of things. First admit to yourself, and truly believe, that the relationship holds no chance of ever becoming romantic. Begin to work through that in the same way you would if a straight man you were romantically interested in wasn't interested in you. You must work your way through all the steps toward acceptance of this reality. Second, you'll need to decide—according to what you know of both your friend and your friendship—if there is room for you to honestly admit your feelings. I would encourage open-hearted candor. If you are honest and admit your feelings—in a way that acknowledges your understanding of how impossible the situation is—then your friendship may well deepen. At the very least you will have made a practical and clear demonstration of the honesty and openness that great friendships are based upon.

One of the things to consider is that if you decide not to address these feelings you're having, then you could be setting yourself up to undermine the friendship in unconscious ways. You might begin to be overly sensitive to perceived slights, reacting to events by way of misinterpreting them according to your suppressed feelings. I mean, I'm certainly not a therapist, but I do know how human emotions work. We tend to project onto others our secret desires and sometimes react to situations as if the other understands what we hold secret. So again, if you go about sharing your feelings in a loving way, you will probably deepen your friendship and, at the very least, prevent yourself from undermining it.

You describe your friend as being totally in tune with your feelings as a woman. Don't you think he would understand these romantic feelings that you're having and that, given the strength of your friendship, he'd be willing to work through them with you? The

one catch is, of course, that although he can participate, the real effort lies with you.

A point that you don't raise is whether or not your
friend is in a significant relationship. Does he have a
boyfriend (or partner, lover, spouse — whatever he calls
him)? If so you should also be respecting the boundaries of this relationship in the same way you would respect the boundaries of a non-gay relationship. Ask
yourself: If I were in love with a straight male friend
and he had a wife, what would I do?

The other significant part of your question ad-
dresses straight men in general. The only advice I can
give you in this regard is to carefully examine the type
of men you are dating. Consider giving up the search
for the perfect man and concentrating instead on creating for yourself — not for anyone else — the perfect
you. In other words, put first things first. Pray, not that
the perfect man appear in your life, but that you are
able to become an incredible person. Understand — really understand — that you are worthy of amazing romantic relationships. I believe that we draw into our
lives that which will help us learn the greatest lessons.
Your experience with straight men may be trying to
teach you to focus first on your own evolution and
then, when the time is right — perhaps when you least
expect it, because you're so happy with yourself and

your life—great romance will follow. And through your amazing friendship with this gay man in your life, you will come to know that men are capable of being creatures with whom you can be in sync.

QUESTION 5: I've been HIV+ for four years. Since finding out I've been taking terrific care of myself. Actually, I've always been health conscious but sero-converting convinced me to really pay attention to overall health. I bought your book *Flawless* and have transformed my body and mind by following your advice on exercise and nutrition. Thank you for such a wonderful book and for inspiring me to work out. My question, however, is about being HIV+. I didn't date for the first three years after I found out that I was positive (unusual but true), and about a year ago I started dating. Most dates didn't even make it to a second dinner; consequently, I never had to deal with disclosing my status to the guy. But I met a guy a couple of months ago that I am crazy about. I'm really ready for a sexual relationship but terrified to address my status for fear of scaring him off. Part of me is afraid to lose him. Part of me is tempted to break up so that I don't have to deal with it. This is tormenting! Any suggestions?

ANSWER 5: Thank you for your compliments on my fitness book. I'm glad that the information in it reaches you and that you've found it helpful with your own process. I wrote it mainly because I believed that sharing what I'd learned through my own experience with exercise, nutrition, and motivation might help others create wonderful changes in their lives. I support you in taking such good care of yourself. You absolutely deserve the best that life has to offer.

As for your dilemma, I believe we must always strive to live each moment with full awareness in order to avoid slipping into easy assumptions about our lives, our priorities, our hopes and dreams. Your situation reminds me of the advice that wise ones have been giving people for centuries: weigh everything in your life—all your actions and thoughts—against your death. Understanding that we are creatures who have a limited life span on this plane has helped tremendous numbers of people separate the essential from the nonsensical.

You have had something come into your life that you could easily interpret in several ways. Your perception of your HIV status affects your reality. It's clear, at least from your letter, that you have chosen to use your status as something of a wake-up call. But there is still a catch, isn't there? You've met someone you're wild about. Obviously you're also taking your time with this man. That can be a great thing. There is nothing wrong with getting to know someone through a slow process. But a lot of your timing seems to be influenced by your HIV status. Ask yourself: To what extent am I coming from a fearful place with this?

Whatever you do, please consider this advice: don't break up with this man just to avoid disclosure. To do so would be to miss an enormous opportunity, one that will impact you and him. We make an error when we believe our life challenges are experiences to avoid automatically. There seems to be a clear signal here for you to dive in and go to a new level of integrating your perceptions of your circumstances with the realities of your life. You say that after three years of not dating and a bunch of first dates, which led to neither sex nor second dates, you are facing this situation. There is something so important happening here. Can you see it? You should listen to that same inner voice that's telling you how wonderful you feel about this guy and trust in that.

Now I am taking a leap here and assuming that, because you are crazy about this man, he must be a good guy, and that he must also be in sync with your feelings. In other words, I assume that the strength of the feelings is mutual. If that is the case then reverse the situation. Put a twist on it. I say this because your letter indicates two things: One is that—by exclusion of information to the contrary—you are assuming that he is HIV negative. The other is that no disclosure has yet been made by either of you. So in reality, he could be negative, he could be positive—who knows? Now go ahead and reverse the situation. Put him in your shoes and you wear his. Would you want him to break up with you to avoid this difficult conversation, probably lying to you (by omission or commission) in the process in order to cover up the real reason for the ending? Now imagine that you are both going through identical processes, scared to confront this situation, worried about what you both perceive to be a potentially devastating conversation.

Do you know what lies at the heart of this matter? Whatever is real cannot be taken away from us. Just as your HIV status can lead your life in so many different directions (acknowledging the reality that these days many people are living asymptomatic for years and years), and could impact your health and perhaps at some point in the future end the life of your physical body, it cannot kill the reality of your soul. That is real. Your soul—you in your truest essence—lives whether you are on this physical plane or not. That is real. It cannot be taken away.

In your romantic situation, if the love is real, if it is to be allowed to evolve, you must put it to this test. If it is real, it cannot be taken away. You must go to this man and have your heart to heart. In your situation, I would spend a couple of days meditating and praying, not for the outcome I wanted, but instead for the highest, most sacred outcome of the situation. Open your heart completely; don't be afraid. Begin by acknowledging to him that you had been scared of the conversation. Be honest and also encourage his honesty, including the possibility that he is not at the same point you are in your life.

You can only save this situation by your actions. If you do nothing, the relationship will most likely end. If you end the relationship to avoid the conversation, well— the relationship will end. So what is the real risk here? You stand to gain so much from this encounter. I hope that it turns out for the highest good of everyone concerned.

QUESTION 6: I write to you anonymously because it is all that I know. Let me explain. I am a forty-four-year-old married man. I have two children and am a successful executive with a very high profile agency. I haven't been with a man in over ten years (that was before I married). I can no longer content myself with this life of denial. I do know that I could not bring myself to leave my wife and children. Ever. Yet my desires continue to intensify. I imagine that it is only a matter of time before I act on this and that terrifies me. I am afraid to lie to my wife, and yet I am unable to imagine living a life this way. I can't, however, imagine telling her that I'm gay. It simply doesn't seem like a viable option. I have followed your career from a distance and respect your choices and would appreciate your thoughts on my predicament.

ANSWER 6: Whenever anyone talks about how unnecessary queer rights issues are, especially as they impact the positive self-identification and the hazards of lifelong suppression, I always think of situations such as yours. It never ceases to amaze me how many men, after years of conscious or unconscious suppression of homosexual desires, begin the initial stages of coming out (even if only to themselves) in their forties, fifties, and sixties. I say that not only to reinforce how destructive the long history of lies and myths has been to so many lives, but also to tell you that your situation is normal and much more common than you might even realize.

I know that you must be scared. You must be worried to death about what you'll do. Yours is indeed a dilemma of tremendous proportions. So many lives will be impacted by your decisions. I pray for the highest outcome of this situation; I am concerned about you, but I am just as concerned about your wife and children.

What is your relationship with your wife like? Is yours a marriage that's based upon total honesty? Only you can know this, but I would ask you to be brutally honest with yourself; cut right to the bone and don't hide anything from your own critical examination.

If you were predominantly heterosexual, would you have an affair with another woman? Would you feel good about that? Would you tell your wife? How would it feel to have such an affair and not tell her? How would having sex with a man, outside of your marriage, differ from having an affair with a woman? These are difficult issues you'll need to address. I do not want to sugarcoat this: if you intend to act in an honest way, you are between a rock and a hard place. There is no getting around that fact. I know that some would recommend that you simply have affairs with men, having only safe sex, and keep them secret from your wife. But I'm not one of those people. I say this knowing that that statement will get me branded by some folks as some sort of repressed, sex-negative, stick-in-the-mud, but I believe that honesty is far more essential to our life path than sexual release. You would not only need to be dishonest with your spouse, but you'd also continuously reinforce to yourself the very destructive idea that your homosexuality is something negative, to be treated as a dirty secret and lied about.

Deceiving your wife would almost certainly guarantee the failure of your marriage, not because she would necessarily find out about your infidelity, but because you would know about it and would almost certainly be compounding cheating with lies. And by failure I don't necessarily mean that your marriage will end in separation or divorce; I mean instead that the trust and foundation of honesty, which solid marriages are based upon, will be violated. You will probably end up seeing and treating the marriage as a failure, and how fulfilled do you think your wife would be? You say that you don't intend to leave her, so I know from that statement that you must love her a great deal and would never purposely want to hurt her, or want to see her life be unfulfilled.

I am going to make the assumption that you want to deal with this situation honestly. Without any hesitation, today, now, find a gay-friendly therapist. You can do this anonymously in a variety of ways. Call a gay hot line in the nearest city, or the next city over, and get referrals. You don't need to give your name for that. Call six or seven therapists; tell them right off the bat that you must initially stay anonymous, but interview them. (This is perfectly normal when shopping for a therapist. Any therapist who tells you it isn't, avoid at all cost.) Ask them the hard questions. Ask them where they stand on gay issues and avoid any counselor who seems wishy washy, or seems like one of these you-can-change-your-sexuality quacks. That's also why a gay hot line or community center would be the place to accumulate names: less chance of being referred to antigay wackos posing as helpful professionals. The last thing you need is someone who is supposed to be helping you, and getting paid to do so, getting the chance to mess with your head. When you've found someone you can work with (and you will—if you can run a successful business you can use that same gumption to find the right counselor), begin a totally honest dialogue about where you are in your life.

The track of your therapy should go along one of two lines. In my opinion, only one of these choices is totally healthy, and if I were in your shoes the choice would be clear—not easy, by any means, but clear.

The first option is to work with your therapist on a system of keeping your homosexual desires on a strictly fantasy level. While not as obviously unhealthy as being unfaithful to your wife, this choice would seem to be an almost total denial of your true self. That in and of itself is a timebomb. The difficulty is that you have begun to work on this issue in your head. How can you now stop it? It's like trying to stop a rock from rolling down a steep hill. You may also have difficulty finding a therapist—one who has your best interests and health in mind—to help you along this track, since it is filled with such a suppression of your true self.

Most likely, on a course such as this, you would end up acting on your fantasies anyway and then you'd be in the same place you would have been if you had simply cheated on your wife. The feedback I've gotten from men in situations similar to yours is that the dishonesty, whether through fantasy or actual sex with another man, leads further down a road of self-loathing, eventually touching every aspect of one's life.

Your second therapy option will be the most difficult, because it involves what you say you don't want. It involves getting healthy with your homosexuality and being completely honest with your wife. I know that you state that this is not an option for you. That's your perspective now. Could you, however, picture a time when this might be possible? Try not to look at the limitations of the situation right now. First, try to get your own mind and heart on a self-accepting track. You might be surprised at what you find a bit down the road. It is important to remember that your situation is similar to most coming out stories, in that a gay person starts off saying that there is no possibility of sharing the information. With time most people find that disclosure is the only path to true identity integration.

I feel that you may be seeing only disaster if you eventually face this issue with your wife. But you cannot predict exactly how she will react to knowing that you are gay. Only the actual experience will reveal that. I can tell you that many men and women who've been in your situation have found satisfying solutions. The solutions were never easy at first, but I've learned that the more honest the approach the more success-ful the outcome. It probably will take a while.

Just to reinforce my opinion that you not have any affair until you are further along the path of self-acceptance—which in and of itself argues for finding that therapist right away—when you come out, you will most likely have a much easier time dealing with your wife, and eventually your family, if you have not been having illicit affairs. The affairs will compound an already difficult situation and perhaps give your wife justification for not dealing with you on the issue.

My hope is that you will look to the underlying spiritual issues involved in your situation. There are strong lessons presenting themselves here regarding truth, fidelity, honesty, and compassion. Whatever you do, please be honest with your wife. In any decision, put yourself in her position and ask yourself how you— on the deepest, most honest level—would want to be treated. My heart goes out to you and your family.

QUESTION 7: I am a twenty-seven-year-old gay man who is having a difficult time merging my sexual orientation with my religious convictions. I was born and raised in Western Canada and am one of six children. We are a very close family and were raised strict Catholics. In the town that I grew up in, religion was a part of life. Unfortunately, homosexuality was not. I've used my Catholicism to get me through some fairly tough times in my life—notably a bout with drugs when I was twenty. My views of religion and God have matured over the years. By that I mean that I have learned to absorb what is comfortable and dismiss what is not. Actually I consider myself to be spiritual rather than religious. But herein lies my struggle.

My Catholic upbringing has played an important and powerful part in defining who I am. As has being gay. I need to figure out how to blend the two. I obviously cannot "give up" being gay, but I do not want to turn my back on my religious upbringing. When I have spoken with friends about this, they often say, "You can't be both gay and a practicing Catholic because the Bible condemns homosexuality." I have never interpreted the Bible that way at all but it seems that so many people do. I have heard that you have strong spiritual convictions. How have you dealt with this? What advice do you have for me?

ANSWER 7: If there is one thing that I know for sure it is that many queers are greater experts on what their religious texts really say than most preachers are. Many of us have to become experts. We have little choice if we want to psychologically survive. It is in learning what the Bible really says about our issues that many of us work through the heartache of being treated as such blatant outsiders.

In the queer rights movement, many times it seems as if we have so little to hold us together, with our sexuality as our only common bond with our queer brothers and sisters. In that we differ from, for example, those involved in the African American civil rights struggle. In that movement, much strength was gained not only through common religious belief, but also from the sense that family members shared the same issues. The support network came closer to home.

If only we, as a queer community, could find a strong, uniting bond, we might find so much more to support about each other. But the fact is that until recently so much of what we have had in common was considered perversion and deviance by the dominant culture (a message we were taught perhaps even more effectively then non-queers were) that we struggle to find a common spiritual context to place our struggle inside of. That's why many queers seem to have turned their backs on anything religious. This makes absolute sense. Why support any institution that says you are automatically condemned?

But our need for spiritual depth does not disappear just because we decide to turn our backs. If anything, my sense is that the need grows greater and that the struggle to reclaim the holy can lead us to a depth of faith that many, who mistake religious dogma for spirituality, might never experience. We must fight our way to true faith. I thank God for that every day.

Because—according to the religion of my youth— I am supposed to be automatically condemned to hell if I'm honest about who I really am, I have had to go through the full cycle of spiritual growth. I look at some people I know, who approach their religion as if God really made them the only chosen people and condemned everyone not like them to hell, and wonder how in the world they can't realize how lost they seem.

One thing that queers should always keep in mind: the Bible was written by men, compiled by men and has been interpreted and reinterpreted thousands of times according to the politics of the translators' time; most of that history has been severely antigay. It is a "chicken and egg" cycle. Which came first, the antigay (translations of) passages, or the hatred of homosexuals?

It is also important to remember that Biblical literalists (those who believe this book to be the literal word of God) pick and choose very selectively which passages to follow and which ones to ignore. The Bible actually has very few mentions of homosexuality—as we understand it—and most are only antigay because of interpretation, not because they were cast in stone. Selective literalism is always a useful tool for anyone actively searching for others to direct hatred toward. We must also constantly remember, in our hearts and minds, exactly how elastic even the most rigid Biblical literalists can be. For example, the Bible has only recently been cleansed—through selective reinterpretation—of its blatantly racist passages. In new versions of the Bible, all that racism disappears, so lo and behold, Bible thumpers can now act as if it never existed at all. It is essential to never forget that in America, an entire religious denomination—the Southern Baptists (which was, by the way, one of the denominations of my upbringing)—was founded specifically because its members supported the enslavement of African Americans. Church elders can try to explain it away, but that is a historical fact. Ironic how one prejudice replaces another. I have to ask myself if denominations won't, one day in the future, be apologizing to gays the way denominations (including Southern Baptists) have begun apologizing to African Americans for their historical support of blatant prejudice.

I do consider myself a spiritual man. As I hope the chapters in the first part of this book showed, my spiritual beliefs color everything about my life. I try to measure every decision through the context of my belief in spiritual justice. I gather hope through my belief in a Higher Power. I find the pure love of God reflected all around me. I have spent a lot of time educating myself on theological issues, mainly because I was raised in such a fundamentalist Christian home culture (I was brought up in a family influenced by the Bible Belt of the southern Midwest and South), a place where it was simply assumed that everyone believed in the infallibility of what the preacher said, and read the Bible for very selective literal passages.

When I came out to myself, I searched for everything I could find that would reconcile my feelings with my upbringing. I read everything I could get my hands on. I began to see the tremendous difference between organized religion and spirituality. I learned that having one did not necessarily guarantee having the other; although sometimes the two did coexist, they could also be mutually exclusive.

My beliefs are simple. We are all children of God (and as I said earlier, I use words such as "children" and "God" knowing that I am operating from very limited language) and are all inherently holy. We are on this earth to reunite with our own true spirits to try to find that essence inside ourselves, using the world to reflect back our true selves. We come here with missions, life circumstances, that help us connect with our true nature, which I believe to be pure love.

I believe that I was born into the circumstances of my life so that I could be reminded that, in spite of hardship, in spite of others' petty hatreds, my soul is one with the divine and can never be separated from that. I structure my life so that I live according to those beliefs. I try to act in an ethical manner. I try to be kind. I strive to be loving and compassionate. And even if my spiritual beliefs end up being completely wrong and there is nothing after this life, just a blank end to a biological accident—even though my faith so clearly demonstrates to me otherwise—I am still attempting to live the right way. Call it ethics, the golden rule, religious or spiritual belief; I think that living the way I do makes me happier, because I feel as if I am trying to make the world a better place to be.

My advice to you is to continue on the path you are on. Spiritual belief is not intended to be easy, in the sense that it doesn't just drop into our laps whole. We must exercise it against the reality of our lives, standing up against the gravity of oppression and finding our own sense of the divine. We must remember that those who have been pioneers of spiritual thought have generally been condemned by fundamentalists of their time. Human beings are resistant to change, especially when they get their explanations from dogmatic teachings, which they are usually told they must find infallible, or run the risk of burning in hell.

As for your religious denomination, there are Catholic groups that are enlightened on gay issues; some are exclusively gay, others are simply congregations that have liberated this issue from the old way of thinking. Your friends who tell you that you cannot be a practicing Catholic and gay are seeing the world through man-made dogma. Their feelings may reflect a dynamic that dominated for a long time, but on a purely spiritual level their opinions are not accurate. I think that you know otherwise. So continue to fully educate yourself and then consider helping them to understand. Many times we learn as we teach.

Do all things with love. Approach your family with love. Come to your church with love. Seek to change your church through loving means. What you are looking for is seeking you. Go out into the world and know that God has a place for you.

QUESTION 8: My partner and I have been together for almost six years. Peter is thirty-six and I am thirty-nine. We are a stable, loving gay couple with great jobs, lots of disposable income, and a beautiful home. When we got together, both Peter and I felt in our hearts that this relationship was special and would last a lifetime. We both still believe that. However, we have recently encountered a problem. Peter wants children. I do not. His paternal instincts have soared and he talks about it constantly. Both his younger brother and sister have recently become new parents and that has only added fuel to the fire. He is constantly trying to convince me that we are ready for this responsibility, we can afford it, it will fulfill us, and so on. Neither of us actually know any gay couples with children and to tell you the truth I have difficulty with what it would be like for the child. But I love my partner and we have always compromised when in any sort of disagreement. This issue, however, feels particularly overwhelming simply because it is so important to him and I am in many ways opposed to the idea.

I am beginning to feel as though Peter will not feel self-actualized without the experience of fatherhood. I have not admitted it to him (and am actually ashamed to admit it to myself), but I don't feel that the world is ready for same-gender co-parenting. By that I mean that I worry about not only the psychological effect on the child but the strain that it would in turn cause my partner and me. What would you suggest that I and others in this type of predicament do?

ANSWER 8: I want to congratulate you guys on having created what sounds like a great relationship. I don't think that we take enough time to acknowledge what an enormous achievement it is for two people of the same gender to create a long-lasting couple relationship. There is a tendency, even in our media, to not fully respect gay relationships. I believe that this comes, to a large extent, from stubbornly maintaining what has traditionally been the queer's place in society. It is slowly changing, because a large number of gay men and women are standing up and saying that the stereotype of the homosexual as a sexual outlaw, living a lonely singular life out on the fringes of society, is generally obsolete and only being held in place by those defending outdated modes of being.

We truly begin to evolve as a culture when we allow others to fully define what works for their own lives and we stop trying to fit everyone into a narrow definition of the correct way of living. Developing into an evolved society means—to me—that we live our lives according to our highest values and let others live according to theirs, so long as we all understand that our rights end where another's begin, and we live our lives in a way that does no one harm.

If we each set out to determine what our values are, then we can begin any question with a clearer prediction of the answer. You and your partner are clearly experiencing a major test of your combined values. The decisions you reach will be important ones, quite possibly influencing the course of your relationship.

Parenting is a major step for any person and any couple. It should be one of the most carefully thought out decisions that anyone makes during a lifetime. In my own life, I've given a great deal of serious thought to this issue. I go back and forth in my feelings. I know that I want children; at times I feel an overwhelming parental urge, one that's so strong that I can taste it. But then at other times, I feel as if my life would still be complete if I didn't raise a child (or children). I seem to vacillate equally between both views; at this point in my life neither one is totally predominant. So I can definitely empathize with both of your perspectives.

On the issue of whether or not it is fair to the child to raise him or her in a gay home, I can only respond that in a gay home it is almost guaranteed that the parent (or parents) have really had to struggle to have kids. It takes some real effort to become a parent when you're queer. And it isn't just that queers must overcome the obvious biological hurdles. Let's face it, a fertile lesbian need only put together some quality sperm, a turkey baster, and good timing to actually get pregnant. Aside from my own jealousy over not having the biological part be so simple for myself, I realize that the difficulties and the questions I face lie more in my own heart and head.

Many of the doubts I've had about how fair gay parenting would be have their roots in the old myths. I must ask myself, which of the lies do I still believe — even on the most subtle level possible? If I can love a child, give that young one a good home and respect his or her humanity, then I can be a loving parent. I came from a home with straight parents who hated each other. I seemed to turn out O.K. I do, however, wonder what life must be like in a home where the parents — regardless of sexuality — really, really love each other and would do anything to protect their family. I try to look to the quality of love parents give to their kids and not to the gender of the parents.

If I decide to become a parent, I will have thought it through from every conceivable angle; I will have had to go through major hurdles, in myself and in the systems that govern parenting. I would make sure that my own partner had equal and sustainable enthusiasm

for the task at hand. I also think it is important to state
that it would not be morally correct for me to lie to get
a baby. I wouldn't be able to pretend to be straight to
adopt. I don't think that any relationship with dishonest beginnings is healthy. The reason that I raise this is
that some people do lie to adopt. There are many ways
to do this; I don't think that I need to list them. All of
them, however, deal with telling lies about sexual orientation to make adoption (or other parenting op-
tions) easier. Having said that, it should be assumed
that what I have to say applies to using a process where
sexual orientation is not hidden.

I do not think that raising a child in a gay home is
wrong. In fact, my sense is that it can be incredibly
right. Having met hundreds of gay families with kids,
I've observed what appear to be a bunch of very
healthy children and teenagers being brought up in
those homes. Will there be situations where gay parents need to go above and beyond what a non-gay
parent would? Absolutely. Gay parents cannot be
hands-off guardians, the way so many straight parents
are. This is another one of those double standards
queers face. Any man and woman—no matter if they
are mature, healthy, well-adjusted, or loving—can
have sex and make a baby, and most likely never have
their parental rights challenged. The gay parent, or

parents, may have child-rearing skills questioned at every turn. They could well face consternation inside and outside the community.

I remember a couple of years ago, when I was single, going through one of my periods where parenthood was again becoming quite tempting. I told one of my friends, an older gay man, that I was considering going forward with having a baby. He was shocked that I'd even consider such a thing, telling me that I should instead get another dog. Yet I had non-gay friends tell me what a great dad they thought I'd make. My point is that gay parents will get support from some, criticism from others; it doesn't follow predictable guidelines.

Here is something to consider: If you truly wanted to be a parent, nothing on earth would be able to stop you. You'd go through anything to have a child. That sounds like where your partner is right now.

You guys need to have some serious heart-to-heart talks. You need to take perhaps the biggest chances with him that you've ever had to take. This is such a serious thing that I would tend to suggest not having any children unless your heart was so compelled that you could climb mountains and cross oceans to do so. If you are not so compelled don't go into the process. Parents should want their children with every fiber of their being.

The whole world might not be ready for same-gender co-parenting, but it is not only possible, it's also happening all around you. Give this matter all the most serious consideration that you can muster. Turn it over to higher guidance. You guys sound as if you may be coming to a crossroads—and a major one at that. Please strongly consider finding a loving counselor, who will guide you through this important decision.

Where do you think your feelings about gay parents come from? Are they based on anything that's been demonstrated to you, or are you tapping into residue of the false myths? I would encourage you to dig here, inside your heart. Inside this issue could be some key steps toward really understanding how you feel about yourself as a gay man. What are your relationships with your birth family like? Do you relate well to any nephews, nieces, or other close kids in your life? Could your decision about parenting just be that you don't want to be a parent and wouldn't even if you were straight?

It is very normal for couples to disagree over fundamental issues like children. The test lies in how differing opinions are dealt with. How will you and your partner defy the odds and continue to make your relationship thrive? Talk, talk, and talk some more. Come to each other with loving open hearts. If you already understand that compromise is necessary to create a healthy marriage, then I'm sure, given time, patience, communication, and perhaps the help of a good therapist, you guys will get through this. Remember that being conscious of the issues can be the first and most essential step toward resolving them.

QUESTION 9: My friend and I (she's lesbian and I'm gay) are writing this letter to you for some sound political advice. We both are twenty and have been good friends for the past year. We met in college and probably became friends because we are both queer and in this town there doesn't seem to be too many of us around. The reason that we are writing is because we have been talking about initiating some sort of gay student council at our college. There aren't any organizations for gay or lesbian students here and we are sure that if we ourselves get involved in the council and figure out a way to implement a gay and lesbian voice, then others might feel more comfortable coming forward to get involved. But we aren't sure how to go about getting involved. More importantly we are uncertain what our "queer agenda" should be on a college campus. We know that as an activist you have been very outspoken and supportive of gay youth and turn to you for some advice.

ANSWER 9: I love the fact that you and your friend want to get involved in creating positive change. A college campus makes an excellent target for your activism. From having spoken on so many campuses, I can tell you that there is no environment in our culture where positive change is more possible. For many students, living on a college campus is the first opportunity they have to make their own choices, to form their own thoughts and opinions. It is the beginning of a true break toward independence. That is why the university campus has long been an important starting ground for social change.

From my own recent experience, I know that when I lectured on campuses about gay rights issues, most times the debate would extend from the campus out into the larger community. Many campuses were changed, although not necessarily because of the lecture, since that was usually a controversial event that came and went. In other words, I wasn't going to be around the day after a speech, no matter how much of a stir my talk caused. The students and campus administrators had to be there to make sure that they could take advantage of any shift, any opening,

whether that meant finally being able to get a nondis-
crimination policy instituted, or shaming an antigay
dean into changing his ways. The changes happened
because students such as you and your friend got involved and stayed involved. So I encourage you both
to find your places in that tradition of activism.

Consider a few things before taking action. First,
are you out to your family? Chances are, if you assume
an activist role on campus, if you're not out now, you
will be. Better to take control now; coming out to family by indirect means (such as being seen on the
evening news) isn't the best way to go about the
process. Would your parents (or whomever is responsible for paying for your schooling, assuming that it isn't
you) find your activism objectionable—again—even if
you've come out to them? Do you have the sort of relationship where you can talk with them honestly and
openly about this?

Let's assume that whatever your family situation
is, you decide to go forward. Congratulations. You
have made such an important step toward living the
ideals that this democracy is based upon. You are
working toward creating positive change.

Your first step should be to do some research.
Find out if there ever has been a gay and lesbian group
of any kind on your campus. Sometimes groups have

formed but disbanded after a while. You could be considering and acting upon an idea that others are also contemplating but for some reason aren't able to act upon. Next, find out if any of the other schools in your area have a group. Is the group successful? Call one of the national gay groups (such as the National Gay and Lesbian Task Force) to find out if there is a campus outreach program from which you can access information. Ask questions. Don't be afraid of rejection or false leads. Dig in and get the information that you need. If you can get some information about the various models of what has worked on other campuses, you don't need to completely reinvent the wheel. Try to network, by any means of correspondence, with other groups. Be pushy and thankful. In other words, don't take no for an answer and be grateful—and express it—when others help you. I would say that whatever course of action you both take, you are definitely on the right track.

One piece of—well, almost parental—advice: don't neglect your classes to do this activism. What you want to do is important, but you are also in school to get an education. It's easy to get caught up in creating activist change and forget your primary purpose.

Finally, your queer agenda should be simple. Gay students (and by extension gay citizens) should be treated equally in all regards; ask for nothing special or privileged. Look only to absolute equal justice. That will mean different things to different people. Part of your mission in doing this is not just the activism itself, but learning what you are made of. What are your beliefs about justice? How do you see queers in our society? This is bigger than it looks on the surface. Follow your highest instincts. Don't be afraid to continue asking for help. Keep your eyes open and be willing to learn and change and grow. What you and your friend are going to do is a great thing.

QUESTION 10: I was born and raised in a very small rural town. About eight months ago I finished high school and moved 1200 miles away to live with my older sister and attend college. The city that I now call home has a huge gay and lesbian population and to tell you the truth it was one of the main reasons that I chose the college that I did. At first I was thrilled to see all the openness and acceptance. Finally, I thought to myself, I can be me for the first time. But what I have encountered so far is a culture that seems sex obsessed. Everywhere I go, everyone I talk to is focused on the next party, getting laid, belonging to the best gym, and doing drugs. Don't get me wrong, I am no saint, but this is just not how I want to live my life.

I've been wondering lately if this is all there is. I may someday want to go back to small town U.S.A. (although some of my gay friends make fun of me and tell me that I have no choice except to live in a city) and I sure don't want to become another lost soul in this city. It might sound clichéd, but I just want to meet a nice guy and settle down. I am starting to feel as though there is something wrong with me. Where do I go to find guys who are interested in the same things I am?

ANSWER 10: I understand what you're saying about growing up in a small rural town. I did too. What a culture shock you must have experienced when you moved to the city, especially a city with such a huge queer population. In the past—and still today, to a lesser degree—it was a rite of passage for many queer men and women to head out of the heartland and into the cities. This migration involved not only going to one of a handful of urban areas, but more specifically involved relocation into one of the gay ghettos. In the past, this move was a survival technique and the ghettos where queers could be out of the closet (even if that was only inside the neighborhood) thrived as centers of gay culture, influencing mainstream culture in ways that queers rarely got full credit for.

For many, the neighborhoods were the first place

where they could be themselves: out, proud, holding hands with a lover in public and so forth. So I never want to give the impression that I am against gay neighborhoods at all. In fact I support the idea that we need strong cultural centers in our cities. The evolution that is taking place now is a post-ghetto boom. Many queers are discovering that, because of the constant work done by so many activists and citizens living out and proud lives, it's quite possible to live wherever they want to live. Based only on anecdotal evidence—from mail I've gotten and people I've met—a lot of times those fleeing the city for the country, or the suburbs, have either become disenchanted with city life, or simply want to live a different lifestyle than an urban environment allows. Many say that ghetto life got them down, that it felt too limited. A number of observers, who enjoy and support life in distinctly queer neighborhoods, think that this move to the 'burbs (or even out of the ghetto into another less traditionally queer part of the city) smacks of some kind of self-hating, sell-out behavior.

Now I can't speak for every case, but I do know that from my observation, nothing could be further from the truth. It is nothing more than pure progress, that every queer in America should applaud. After all, this was supposed to be one of the main goals of the early gay rights movement: the ability for gay men and women to live full, rich lives anywhere they wanted to live. When someone says that a ghetto should be all we know, because to live elsewhere is an act of self-hatred, they argue for limitation, they judge pejoratively, they try to tell people how to live, and they condemn others who disagree. Do you see the difference in the two world views?

I say, let's build a country where queers can live anywhere and everywhere. That's a concept that's open to enormous possibility. Those who criticize anyone who doesn't want to live in a ghetto are closing down and limiting life's possibilities, and need to examine their hearts to see what makes them want to create boundaries on other peoples' choices.

Our cities have some problems, but they are broad-based and not just limited to queer culture. But that being said, our urban queer cultures have some very definite issues to deal with. Nihilism is running rampant. Severe drug abuse (not just casual use, but hardcore abuse) feels woven into the fabric of many lives in our ghettos. Even in the midst of a continuing health crisis, bathhouses and sex clubs are flourishing (even if in a slightly different form than the last generation of such clubs). That's not a negative comment about sex, but instead a concern about how severe drug and alcohol abuse, combined with an "oh-the-hell-with-it" attitude toward sex with multiple strangers, is going to play out. To me, and to more queers than many of the watchdogs of our culture want to admit, this does seem like a bunch of lost souls screaming out for help. That's so frustrating, considering the gigantic steps forward queers are taking right now.

I think that it shows how much the lies and false myths still rattle around in the back of many queer minds; how much the residue of self-loathing is still present even in our places of freedom. It shows how true the concept is that the only true freedom lies within our souls, and that we will never be whole unless we begin to honestly heal our wounds and stop wearing nihilistic behavior as if it were a badge of courage. It points the way for the next generation of strategy in our struggle. How do we reach those who just don't give a damn about themselves? Perhaps we can't.

I know I've answered your question indirectly. I did it that way to try to demonstrate that you don't need to live any other way except according to your own highest guidance. Don't let anyone ever tell you otherwise.

There is an issue here that you should look at. You're young. People your age—queer or non-queer— like to party. It's a pretty natural rite of passage. What you need to determine for your own life is where your comfort lies. No matter where you live, superficial party-hearty lifestyles aren't all there is to gay life. Part of the problem might be where you're meeting people. Are you meeting them at bars? People go to bars to party. On the surface there does seem to be heavy emphasis on superficial things in our culture, but you may need to dig deeper. In life, we tend to find whatever it is that we look for.

Think about this: If you were a straight guy and wanted to meet a woman to settle down with, where would you go? Would you go to a singles bar where everyone there is probably trying to get high or get laid? Or would you seek out other sources to meet someone who wanted what you wanted out of life?

Also, I don't want to give you the idea that you can't meet quality men in bars. I know of several great romances—some of which have turned into long-term relationships—where the partners met in bars. However, in every single one of these cases, the guys didn't go to the bars looking for a relationship; they all seemed to accidentally run into a wonderful guy just when they weren't looking at all. You just never know.

You live in a big city with a huge gay population. I can guarantee you that the population there is quite diverse. You might just be looking east to see the sunset—if you know what I mean. Change your perspective. Also one small piece of advice that I can offer, which reflects something I said above—do with it what you may: During my entire life, I have never found a relationship (whether just serious dating, or settling down for the long haul) when I was looking for one. If you want to meet someone terrific, who shares your values, work on becoming the best person you can be. Believe me when I say that you will be able to have the life that you want if you just trust that it is possible and try to live according to your highest ideals.

QUESTION 11: I am a twenty-seven-year-old gay man who just celebrated my one-year anniversary of coming out to my family. I am happy to tell you that it has been a positive experience. They had some difficulty at first but we worked through it easily and it has really improved my relationship with them.

For the past seven months I have been dating a guy and our relationship has gotten very serious. We are moving in together next month and we are both thrilled with the thought of living together. I have told my parents and they are supportive. Both my mom and dad have met my boyfriend and seem to like him. The problem is that they have told me that when we visit them (and we are planning on spending a week with them at Christmas), we will have separate bedrooms. I flipped out at both my parents, telling them that they are being homophobic and hypocritical. First of all, I am a twenty-seven-year-old man who is living with my boyfriend. Then, for God's sake, they know that we are moving into a one-bedroom apartment and will be sleeping together every night.

How can I tell my boyfriend that my parents are accepting of our relationship but that we must sleep in separate bedrooms when we visit them? The whole thing has really made me angry and I am thinking of canceling our Christmas holiday. I thought they were so liberal minded. What am I supposed to do with this mess?

ANSWER 11: Congratulations. You should definitely celebrate your one-year coming-out anniversary. Telling your parents is such a major step—one that's often filled with so many layers of worry, imaginary conversations, imaginary outcomes—that it is easy to overlook the fact that the coming out actually takes time to become fully integrated into every aspect of life. You and your parents have more work to do. No matter how positive your experience was with them, their reaction to your bringing a boyfriend home points out that there's still a ways to go.

One of the key things to understand in this process is that there are no general answers to coming out questions, because you just never know how individual parents are going to react to the information that one of their children is gay. And even if the initial reaction to the coming out seems positive, there can be many stumbling blocks along the way. You and your parents seem to have reached one of those blocks. This sounds as if your parents had little problem with the abstract notion of your being queer, but having a boyfriend makes it undeniably real. Your parents have probably reached a wall of discomfort in one, or both, of their personal comfort zones. The discomfort could well be picturing you and your boyfriend in bed together. Their "little boy" is going to be sleeping with another man, and it may be freaking them out some.

You don't say whether or not you have siblings, or whether any of those siblings are straight. Let's pretend for a moment, though, that you have a straight sister (let's say she's twenty-eight years old). She has a boyfriend of several months. Her circumstances are similar to yours—they've just gotten serious, moving in together, one-bedroom apartment, and so forth. How would your parents react to this? Don't know? Ask them. Sit them down, just the three of you, and in the most loving way you can, ask them. If you were straight and the situation were similar, would they make you and your girlfriend sleep in separate bedrooms? Use your best skills to get them to answer you honestly. You're twenty-seven; speak to your parents adult to adults. If they aren't willing to speak with you as an adult, that could be a big part of the problem.

I have observed that many times—even given positive coming out experiences—families treat a gay member as a kind of suspended adolescent and not as a full adult; this is more times than not a subtle, underlying attitude. Let's face it, our societal traditions have generally said that someone becomes an adult by taking a wife or husband (with the assumption of heterosexuality) and having kids. Even though you are twenty-seven, your gayness could be suspending you in your parents' minds as some sort of abstract teenager. You may need to address this situation first. Your parents must treat you as an adult. You must go to them acting as one. A big key in acting as a mature adult is patience. Remember that you probably had many years to fully come out to yourself. Your parents have had a year. Your levels of process are at dramatically different stages.

What you will need to establish is whether or not your parents are willing to move on this issue. There are some things to ask yourself: How integrated into your family life is your boyfriend? Have your parents met him? If they have, do they like him? Has he made an effort to get to know your family? I'm wondering if this is one of those classic situations where the parents simply feel protective of a child and think that no one is good enough for their baby, and therefore they unconsciously act in a way that shows subtle disapproval.

If this is simply a matter of your parents not wanting the two of you to sleep together and they also already are at least acquainted with your boyfriend, and would allow a non-gay offspring to stay in the same bed with a significant other, then you and your parents have work to do. You can only do your part. Again, do it in a mature way. Be honest, be loving, be respectful. Understand that they might not be open to changing their minds right now. You'll need to make some decisions based on this.

If they are simply unwilling to budge and you have tried everything—and I mean really tried everything—you may need to consider the first stages of some tough love. I don't believe that our relationships should be treated any differently than non-gay relationships. You may need to prove your point with your parents and celebrate the holidays in your own home, with your boyfriend. If this is the case, invite your parents to come to your celebration.

With time and patience on your part, I'm sure that you will be able to resolve this situation. I hope that it is resolved in a way that brings your family closer together and helps everyone concerned evolve in the most positive ways imaginable.

QUESTION 12: I've been living with my partner of twelve years since I was twenty-two. John was my first lover as I was somewhat of a late bloomer. John, on the other hand, realized he was gay at a very early age and had numerous sexual experiences as well as two serious relationships prior to meeting me. When we first got together I was encouraged to date other men—to sow some wild oats, as they say. I was smitten and that soon turned to love. Consequently I chose not to sleep with anyone other than John.

With some reservations (on his part) we moved in together. For the first year of our relationship, he expressed anxiety that I would eventually need to be with other men. He strongly felt that one day I would regret limiting myself to one partner and that I would need to act on that. I guess he wanted me to do that sooner rather than later. I, on the other hand, was convinced that I would always be contented with having only one sexual partner. Our sex life was terrific and I couldn't imagine wanting to be with anyone else. He conceded, and those discussions ended over ten years ago.

But now, I am afraid, John was right. I've been repressing these urges for a while now and although I have not acted on them, they are very real and very strong. Our sex life is still good, but after twelve years together it isn't what it used to be. I'm terrified to discuss it with him because I don't want to hear "I told you so, why didn't you listen to me then?" Our relationship is, for the most part, a very loving and healthy and supportive one. Yet these feelings are getting stronger. I don't want to mess up twelve wonderful years but I can no longer pretend that these thoughts aren't real. A good friend suggested that I write to you for advice.

ANSWER 12: The situation that you find yourself in must be very painful for you. First of all I must say that you and John are very lucky that you found each other and that you have had, from what I can see, twelve great years together as a couple. I would encourage you to count your blessings for this. This world can indeed be very hard on queer couples.

As a broad community, we seem to be trying to clearly define the parameters of our relationships in a world that only recently began reflecting back any images at all of what it meant to be in a same-gender couple. And in a large sense, our queer culture's media images have generally been—until pretty recently—saturated with images of queers as mostly single or, even in committed relationships, sexually nonexclusive. These images may reflect some lives, but certainly not all. I've always felt that there's been a strong dichotomy between the real life of many queers and the media images that come at us, which treat us all as singular, completely sexual entities. Many of our media images—which now seem to be shifting to more accurately reflect our lives—were developed from a mindset that viewed sexual promiscuity as the only choice a real queer could make in life. But that is changing and was never, ever the only way queers lived their lives in the first place.

You should be proud of the fact that you guys made a decision to be sexually exclusive and stayed with that choice—you communicated truthfully with each other and then stuck to your ideals. For many, a commitment to monogamy is not an easy decision to make, and it is certainly not a simple concept to live up to.

The feelings that you are having are very normal. I hope that you understand this. You do, however, have to face what will be a disturbing revelation to your partner. I empathize with your dilemma, but must encourage you to be, above all else, completely honest with John. Your relationship will not grow—at the deepest, highest spiritual levels—from dishonesty of any kind, especially dishonesty regarding a central relationship issue such as sexual fidelity.

My sense is that you must put your fear that John will say "told ya so" into a better perspective. I don't get the idea from your letter that this has been a continuous topic of conversation for twelve years. How long has it been since the topic even came up?

So you've only been with one man in your life. There are some who would call that ideal and deeply romantic (many couples have big-time issues revolving around past lovers). Others would say that you cut your life short by not having more sexual experiences. But you see, all that's important here is how you feel and how you balance those feelings with your relationship with John. That's the heart of the matter—not whether the people around you (especially queer friends so full of good advice on exactly what you should do) think you should fool around, forget about it, or whatever.

Here is what is clear to me. You have the opportunity to take your relationship with John to a deeper level. If you have the courage to face this situation honestly and John is willing to go there with you, you guys could become closer than you've ever been. You have twelve years of solid history to back up any decisions you make. My guess is that the only way you guys have gotten this far is by communicating with each other honestly. I hope that you'll continue that and perhaps find even deeper levels of communication.

You've got to go to John in the most loving way possible. Don't simply go to him with a problem; instead, think long and hard about potential solutions and be prepared to discuss these with him. If you delay initiating this conversation with him—and chances are that it will continue into an ongoing dialogue— you run the risk of letting your emotions build to the point of explosion. You might pick a fight, just to be able to blurt out that the relationship isn't working and that you're going to have an affair. These things happen. You would be better served by being proactive. Confront the situation head-on.

Now as far as outcomes are concerned, there is no way I can advise you on whether or not you should act on your fantasies. That's going to be up to you and John to resolve in an honest and loving way. The reason I wrote earlier in this answer about the queer community's historic tendency toward buying into media images that reflected nonexclusive sexuality is that I want to avoid putting any pressure on you (and by extension you and John) to act in any direction; there is no absolute right or wrong here, no one true way to be a real queer, or a queer couple. We have the right and the responsibility to each define our own lives and relationships. Some will be monogamous, some won't, just as some people will remain single and some will marry.

Also, remember that things change and, although that can be frightening, it can also be a catalyst for growth. Whatever you do, be honest with your partner and act in the highest, most loving way toward both him and yourself.

QUESTION 13: I guess that it's true that all generations carve out their own belief system. My sense is that a generation always differs, either slightly or radically, from the one that preceded it as well as the one that will follow it.

As a nineteen-year-old man who has been "out" since junior high school, I'm a little confused about how I fit into any sense of "community." I've been sexually active for a couple of years. I've dated guys and I've dated girls and have slept with both, and I've had equally satisfying emotional and sexual relationships with both. When I go out, I go to "gay" clubs, "straight" clubs, and clubs where anything goes and no one gives a shit who you are with (in my opinion, the way the world should be). I find myself getting more and more annoyed and perplexed when asked, "So, what are you?" I'm told that because I sleep with guys, I must be "queer." I'm also told that because I sleep with girls, I must be "straight" and that the queer thing is just a phase. Then there are those who think they've got me all figured out and toss me into the "bisexual" group. Hell, I hate all the labels and do not identify with any one of them. Why do older generations seem to need to box everyone into a neat, tidy little compartment with a label firmly affixed to it? That being said, I still haven't got a clue as to what to tell all those people out there who will eventually ask that awful question.

ANSWER 13: Rather amazing how humans have the need to label everything, isn't it? It can be especially frustrating when you feel as if no cut-and-dried category fits you or the way you view your life. In an ideal world there wouldn't be any need at all for the labels you so despise. I think you realize that it's not just older generations that get caught up in pigeonholing people. It seems to be just a natural human tendency that is probably rooted in our evolutionary or genetic makeup. Humans tribalize. We have always thrived on "us vs. them" thinking. Maybe the issues you raise show us how our next phase of human evolution should unfold. In a perfect world we would each get to structure our lives as we choose, without judgment from others.

There are a few interesting points that your question raises. To me your question exposes both how far queer rights have come and how much more progress we have yet to make. I see your frustration, in other words, as a sign of hope.

It wasn't too many years ago when someone in your position wouldn't even have the luxury of challenging such radical labels and identifications. The entire concept of someone being able to be so self-accepting, so out there, so sure of what they want, is rather new in our modern outlook toward sexuality—at least in our honest outlook toward sexuality. In generations past a guy like you may well have married a woman and had secret sexual liaisons with men, never disclosing the queer side of his life. Now you live in a culture where the possibility of having a queer identity exists. That's something to be grateful for. I know that it will sound like such an old-guy thing to say, but please appreciate that the world has shifted dramatically during the past couple of decades—and it has shifted in ways that enable you to live an honest, open life, with an ever-decreasing need to fear any violence or negative consequences.

Now, no matter how you see your sexuality, you're still queer—at least according to my definition of that word. I call myself queer because my sexuality does not fit neatly into the narrow definitions of the dominant culture. Neither does yours. I don't know whether you're bisexual or not. It seems as if you simply date whomever you're attracted to, no matter which gender that person is. Believe it or not, it wasn't too long ago when queers made very harsh judgments about those in your position. Queers called it confusion, being closeted, lying, and a bunch of other pejorative labels. My sense is that this derogatory outlook grew out of the oppression and history of the closet. The closet so dominated queer history that there may have never been room to visualize what the world might look like for someone who was never influenced by it.

Do you understand that your having come out in junior high was unheard of until recent years? You are a pioneer. Be patient and let everyone catch up. I would say—for fear of labeling further—that you're post-queer.

However, there are a couple of things that I'd love for you to consider. The queer rights fight goes on; we are not even halfway there yet. If you dated and eventually married a woman, you'd have all your rights. Do you follow me? If you dated and wanted to marry a guy, you wouldn't have your rights. If you wanted to ask a guy out on a date, or wanted to have sex with him, you'd be acting on your queer side—right? You've got a queer side to your nature. You've got to face that.

So even if you skip past labels, I hope you will understand that there is still more progress to be made. I know that you're sick of being labeled, but that's just human nature. Work within yourself to understand this, while simultaneously helping the people in your life to understand that you're breaking new ground. When you're ahead of your time, it sometimes takes a lot of patience, a lot more than you might think you have, waiting around for everyone else to catch up. Just don't take for granted that a massive evolution and revolution has had to take place for you to even have the freedom and understanding to be so frustrated.

QUESTION 14: As I sit here writing this letter to you, I realize that I may end up fueling your fire. However, I still need to tell you what is on my mind. I am writing to tell you that there are many of us out here that you simply do not represent. Many of us disapprove of your radical opinions and lifestyle. You, like many gay activists, seem hell-bent on changing the world and I am writing to tell you that I wish you'd leave well enough alone. Stop drawing attention to something that doesn't benefit from being scrutinized.

I have no desire to anger you or ignite your endless energy to change things, but I do want to express my view. Gay men and women have always been around, and we always will be. But having your face and your name in print will not change anything. You simply end up drawing more attention to gay people, which results in even more disapproval and hatred directed our way.

Instead of advocating that young men and women come out and live their lives as "open, proud citizens," you should be telling them to accept who they are and just go on with their lives quietly. I have done that my whole life and have done very nicely for myself. My lover and I have done very well in our careers because no one knows that we are gay. At home we can be who we are—in public no one needs to know.

So, some unsolicited advice: forget about gay marriages, forget all this wasted energy waving banners, carrying placards, and writing books. No one wants to be born gay, but we are and we should just quietly accept it, live our lives, and stop trying to fight a battle that can't be won.

ANSWER 14: How do I even begin to address how deeply I disagree with the things that you say? I guess that I must begin, since I was raised in a home where good manners were required, by reciting the old cliché, "You're entitled to your opinion."

O.K., first things first. I will never join anyone in defending the closet. Period. It is a vile trap that sucks the soul out of far too many lives. The institutions that have required queers to hide their true natures have been around too long, and—if you will excuse me for being so bold—have remained in place, in no small part, through the cooperation of a breed of closeted queers, who think that anyone who doesn't hate themselves as much as they do is unforgivably radical. Your lifestyle seems to revolve around a central core of falsehood. And that's never a healthy way to live.

We come out of the closet these days so that in the future we can simply live our lives, but live them on our own terms, not the terms of historical bigotry or cooperation with that system of prejudice.

Your belief system is totally based on the premise that being gay is a negative thing. I could not disagree more. I see my gayness as a tool for the evolution of my soul. For me a major part of that evolution is coming to terms with the fact that I was raised with lies about who I am. So were you. The difference is that I want to change those lies to truths in the minds of good people around me—and probably more essentially, in my own mind and heart. I want to engage in this soul struggle; you sound as if you want to avoid it. But avoiding struggle creates results quite similar to what happens when you worry about something awful that you imagine will happen in the future: you suffer while you worry—as if the events you imagine are real. In much the same way, you create more negative energy in your life by sustaining a closeted lifestyle than if you were to simply, but bravely, face the truth of who you are. When the closet, like imaginary worries, is left behind, most of the things that we think are going to be disasters end up being nothing, or at least easy to deal with.

Going about our lives quietly is all well and good, if we aren't living lies. Also I might add an observation that many, who've led deeply closeted lives and then come out, have shared with me: you might think that you're hiding something, but it's a good bet that everyone in your life knows you're queer without you even saying a word. The tension that you put around sustaining this gigantic lie reveals your secret for you. Others are simply cooperating in your lie.

I don't know what the quality of your life has been, nor do I know what sort of life you and your lover have together. I can only go from the tone of your letter which seems to indicate that you guys are not only closeted at work, but probably also to your families and to all but a small circle of people in your life. To me this seems a sad way to live. What kind of respect do you and your lover have for each other when you pretend for others that your relationship doesn't exist? Do you really feel as if your life isn't equal to that of the non-gay people around you? This is what you say when you stay so deeply closeted and defend your position by attacking those who live with greater honesty. I know that I seem harsh. But my sense is that the most loving thing I can do in this case is not handle your defense of a dishonest life with kid gloves, but instead tell you that there is no way to turn back the clock on the world, returning to the sort of secretive double lives that queers had to live in order to survive for so long.

From the bottom of my heart, I wish that you and your lover would find a progressive, gay-positive counselor to speak with. I wish, in addition, that you would search your heart to see that you were told lies about who you are and that life does not have to be the way you see it. Your life sounds as if it is sad.

Also I take exception to your statement that no one wants to be born gay. I may have struggled throughout most of my adult life to fully, at the most spiritual level possible, accept my gayness, but I thank God every day for making me queer. I wouldn't trade the soul lessons I've gained through my gayness for anything, and if I weren't gay, I wouldn't be in the magnificent relationship I'm in with a wonderful man. Get it? A *man*. How can I wish away my queerness, or not embrace it and say that I truly love the man I am with? Don't you see the self-loathing in your arguments? Please, please, please get help. Life doesn't have to be how you see it. I guarantee it. And by the way, as to the battle that we can't win—according to you—we already are winning it.

QUESTION 15: When in God's name are you going to join the winning team? Stop calling yourself an activist and start doing the real work. All you queer men and women out there who do nothing more than whimper about how we need equal rights sicken me. Queers need equal rights like we need a hole in the head. Our goal, as queers, shouldn't be "equal rights." Our goal shouldn't be recognized marriages. Our goal shouldn't be to be able to legally adopt children and blend our families with the heterosexual families at PTA gatherings. We are wasting our time and energy modeling our lives after breeders. Making these things our goals makes you, and everyone like you, a sellout.

What we need our "activists" to do is embrace the real queer community. We are queer, we are outsiders. Always have been. Always will be. And that is the best scenario. If we go "inside" and sit at that table, we simply become members of that mess that heterosexuals foolishly call a life.

I am proud of my outsidership. It is a great club. It is a private club. It should remain that way. So stop with all this conservative goal setting. Enough model-ing ourselves after the breeders. Be queer and be proud, but for God's sake don't sell out.

ANSWER 15: Your question reminds me, in many ways, of the question preceding it. You just happen to be filtering it through a superficially opposite lens.

Masked behind your manufactured disagree-ments with me, and attacks on who I am, is the accu-sation that if people don't do things your way, they are hurting themselves and others. There are underlying accusations that I am somehow telling others how to live, but instead, my perception is that, just like the man who says that the one proper way to be queer is to stay in the closet, you say that the only way to be queer is to do things as you see them. In other words, you hide behind your accusation that I am telling others how to live, while simultaneously telling others how to live. You call yourself an outsider, yet demand confor-mity. I'm trying to say this in the most compassionate way possible, but I must admit that this whole idea that there is one true way to be a real queer is silly and ul-timately destructive; it keeps us off course.

Also this whole notion of labels really holds our movement back, not because there aren't conservative and liberal queers who have differences of opinion, but because labels are often used in a pejorative manner, as a means of attempting to render someone else's opinions irrelevant. And in our movement, the labels can be extremely inaccurate.

Our fundamental goal should be getting our full civil rights; a major stepping stone toward that goal is for us to encourage each other, no matter what our differences, to become well-adjusted people, who just so happen to live in a diverse society. Can't you see that we as queers have the opportunity to show the world how people with such stark differences can get along and live in a workable civilization? Are you so caught up in staking out some territory where you feel right and holier than thou that you can't see that your attacks on me are demonstrations of how intolerant you are being?

We live in a diverse world. It was always my understanding that the queer rights movement was supposed to be celebrating that diversity, not saying the words and then doing exactly the opposite. Please think about this.

Contrary to what you might believe, we are not enemies. I am not a "sellout" because I want to be able to live as a first class citizen in my country, or because I don't live exactly as you live. How is what you're doing all that different from what someone who's anti-gay does to all queers? I hope you'll begin to shift away from a focus on difference and begin to look harder for the places where our common interests intersect.

I hope that you will reject the notion that we are a people divided along such rigid ideological lines. How much of your hatred stems from oppression, how much from lies? You sound trapped to me; I don't say that because we disagree, but because of how you approach issues and express such deep-seated fear of difference.

Those who are working for gay rights, but with whom you happen to disagree, are not sellouts. Can't you see that if you go around calling others names, you not only disrespect their humanity, but also ultimately reveal how much you dislike yourself? And what's with calling all straight people "breeders" in such a mean-spirited way? How do you expect to be treated with anything except contempt by non-queers when you call them names and are so blatantly heterophobic?

I know that those who function along rigid ideological lines are not known for their introspection, but I hope that you will prove to be an exception to that notion. You can be an outsider, but your right to be that is directly tied to others' rights to be themselves also—even if that self is radically different from who you see yourself as being.

QUESTION 16: I know that you believe in the right of gays to get married. I am in total agreement with that. In fact I think that it is a no-brainer for all queers to want this right. It confuses me, though, how some very outspoken queers, who call themselves radical, criticize the concept of marriage as some archaic, archconservative institution. I've even heard activists claim that gay marriage is a co-option of a tradition that is completely sexist and homophobic, and that anyone who supports it—if they are queer—is a self-hating sellout. Also—and I suppose along that same line of thinking—I've heard a couple of my more radical friends describe you as a conservative and a sellout. When I press them for reasons why, they usually fall back on your support for gay marriage. What gives?

ANSWER 16: The first time that I read in a gay newspaper that my opinion about something or other was considered by the writer to be extremely conservative (and given the context of the remarks, it wasn't intended as a compliment), I felt as if a rusty, dull butcher knife had just been dragged across my stomach. Conservative? Extremely conservative? Where did that one come from? I wondered. It wasn't that the term in and of itself was all that insulting. It just wasn't accurate. And it was used in such a pejorative manner. It was meant to wound, to discount my efforts; it was a code word for misguided. That was probably the first time I gave serious consideration to exactly what those seemingly polar opposite terms—conservative and liberal—actually mean in the queer world, a world of underdogs and outsiders.

I began wondering whether or not the entire concept of queer rights could ever truly succeed given the fact that so many of the movement's journalists seem to spend more energy tearing down gay activists, over what could only be construed as quibbles, than fighting enemies. I mean, what is that all about anyway—this need to condemn our own? Self-love? Doubtful. Sophistication? Not from where I sit. I don't consider myself to be at all naive, yet I don't find myself needing, much less craving, to destroy others to build myself up. And then I realized something amazing. I was getting caught up. I was responding to old-style thinking with old-style responses. I couldn't be insulted on a personal level, just because I felt misunderstood. I had to go deeper.

Out in the world, at lectures or in letters, I am constantly asked what I think about this "conservative" activist or that "liberal" activist. I have been wondering for quite some time if the old labels even apply to what we are going through. So much of our labeling seems to get it backward, ignoring how dramatically the low rumbling earthquake of change has already shifted our landscape.

A simple question rises up, a question deeper than superficial labels. Is this a movement that can survive and succeed, in spite of being made up of such a diverse group of people, and can we win our freedom and still hold so many emotionally charged and divergent points of view? Yes. We can. But we must break free of the old style of discourse. Divide and conquer will not work for our people. It will take more. That is our opportunity, if we look past this fog. We must see that our definitions don't fit the old traditional molds, and when we measure our issues with outdated yardsticks, we get pulled off course.

How do we break past the old style of labeling and divisiveness? By looking straight into the heart of the matter. If we have the courage to look at things for how they really are and not simply accept the vapors as stone, we will have the opportunity to make a massive breakthrough toward enlightenment. That is why some resist. Change is hard. Those who have an investment in the old way of looking at things will resist this change in perspective with all their might. But we already are changing; we must have the courage to recognize how much the old definitions and divisions have become obsolete.

What we need here are some clear definitions. I've always understood that the very definition of conservative revolved around the maintenance of long-standing, traditional points of view—conserving an idealized, specific world order. I also thought that the term liberal meant the liberation from what had long been held as traditional and therefore conservative, and—perhaps more essentially—that liberalism indicated a willingness toward inclusion. My understanding of the traditional definition of liberalism was that it was supposed to involve an attempt to include others and question traditional assumptions that may have been entrenched even in the face of change. What I've begun to wonder is this: Is it reasonable for queer citizens to remain chained to traditional—and therefore, by definition, conservative—definitions of what is liberal or conservative? That remains to be seen.

I find it rather humorous that I am labeled by some self-described radicals as being extremely conservative. I should share a couple of points of my personal history. If I had to categorize my own political leanings, I'd say that I've always been a liberal Democrat (that is, in the traditional, conservative sense of the definition). Because of one simple act—having had a gay marriage, years before marriage became the issue du jour of the queer movement—I was branded by some as being extremely conservative. This was the worst of all possible things to be, according to these cultural gatekeepers—a sure sign of self-hate and political naiveté. In short, I was, without benefit of evidence, proclaimed a sellout, an assimilationist pig. This would sometimes be followed by the simultaneous accusations that I was both dumb as a rock (and who did I think I was in the first place, violating my place in the queer universe as a piece of meat?) and that I was trying to tell other queers how to live. Now, I tend to think of myself as dumber than some, smarter than others, but not really taking either characterization all that seriously. But the accusation that I was somehow trying to tell others how to live? That one made me mad.

I tried to remember the things I'd said. I recalled saying in interviews things such as, "Stand up for who you are and let others be themselves too." So long as we aren't hurting each other, we should each recognize that our differences make the world richer. It is in striving for sameness—in any direction—that we become bankrupt as a society. It is through the striving for a homogenized society that oppression of outsiders truly thrives.

There was a delicious irony in having those who want to narrow the choices that queers can make in structuring their lives, by condemning and demonizing whatever doesn't fit the accuser's own limited agenda, say that I was trying to tell other queers how to live. The accusers always seemed perfectly content to try to clearly define what made someone a "real" queer, and therefore, in ways both subtle and blatant, they were telling others how to live their lives. Perhaps accusing others of doing the very thing you yourself are doing—telling people how to be a real queer, and condemning anyone whose opinion differs from that definition (even if you only suspect it does)—is a way to deflect attention away from your own blatant hypocrisy. Who knows? I do know that this entire process was a test of how well I was able to practice my ideals. Could I face judgment and what I perceived to be limited, narrow points of view and still stay on course? Could I face this anger and what appeared to be such blatant hypocrisy, without resorting to retaliation? Could I reject indulging in the techniques that I felt were outdated beyond measure?

But I digress. The real issue that I'm trying to get at—beyond the hypocrisy of doing exactly what you accuse and condemn others of doing—is, what constitutes being liberal or conservative in the queer rights movement? Certainly many of the writers working in the gay media would most likely define themselves as liberal; this may be why the term conservative gets tossed around like a schoolyard cuss word. But are those who resist the shifting importance of issues in the gay community—away, for example, from issues revolving exclusively around sexual matters—are those people truly liberal? Aren't they simply trying to conserve what has traditionally been the gay person's place in our society: singular entities, with no family ties, and certainly nothing resembling responsibility to anything beyond instant gratification and the glorification of outsidership above all else? Sounds conservative to me—very conservative in fact.

So this question arises again: Does the traditional, and therefore conservative, meaning of liberal and conservative still apply to queer civil rights? Not only that, but what is it in human nature that compels us to categorize our issues in narrow either/or definitions, when in reality most situations contain elements of both tradition and new thought? Of course, experience in the real world, and not simply an idealized version of the world, exposes that very little of life is actually lived according to rigid ideological categorization; that in fact most people tend to live their lives according to a blend of conservatism, liberalism, and all points in between throughout a lifetime. Most people spend their lives conserving certain beliefs, liberating themselves from other beliefs that no longer work, and going back and forth between the two on a continuing basis.

But I want to go back for a moment to the issue of gay marriage, since it is a concept that seems to confound so many old-style queer activists. To listen to some queer activists, many of whom would describe themselves as being radical and liberal, one might assume that most queers oppose the right to have gay relationships legally recognized at a level exactly equal with non-queer relationships. Only a few months ago, a journalist from a regional gay paper—in a state where the legislature is attempting to legally ban queer marriages—claimed that most gay and lesbian folks didn't want the right to get married, because marriage was filled with sexism and was, in general, a homophobic institution. Really? Huh? No wonder the radical right thinks that queers are the perfect scapegoats; we have leaders out arguing why we don't deserve—or, supposedly, even desire—the full spectrum of civil rights.

Now it doesn't take a genius to figure out that

marriage was, for a very long time, a sexist institution, where women were seen mostly as a man's property. It is also not difficult to prove that marriage, as it has been traditionally defined, has been homophobic. It has, after all, excluded queers from marrying someone of the same gender, and was therefore a bigoted institution. But to automatically leap to the conclusion that allowing queer couples to have legally recognized spousal rights, equal to what is available to non-queer couples, would somehow spread sexism and homophobia throughout the gay community is ridiculous. To begin with, how is a marriage between two queer men or women homophobic? I wish someone would explain this one with an answer more reasonable than screaming, "You're a right-wing sellout!" There is no way to explain how a gay marriage is homophobic. It would be, by its very nature, the exact opposite of homophobic. And how does a couple of women who love each other, promising to do their absolute best to care for each other through thick and thin, contribute automatically to an environment of sexism? The sexism of a traditional heterosexual marriage has been absolutely a major part of the institution for a very long time, but even that's no longer a given. How does one woman automatically hold sexist ownership of the woman she pledges her love to?

Queers who oppose the community's fight for equal marriage rights always claim that the concept is an extremely conservative institution, a co-opting of tradition. This, of course, is off base, as there is no established tradition to conserve. In fact, if you discussed the issue of gay marriage with most people in the heterosexual mainstream—as I have continuously done during the past several years—you would find that many consider it to be a few steps beyond liberal; most non-gays consider gay marriages to be downright radical, as a matter of fact. So how is it that gay critics of those who assert gay people's right to have their relationships legally (and yes, perhaps spiritually) recognized, consistently act as if those who want and demand this right are archconservatives, and are somehow selling out the gay rights movement? Aren't those critics actually the true conservatives in this matter? They are, after all, arguing that it is the tradition of queer outsidership that would be surrendered by selling out to marriage. Aren't the gay critics of queer marriage actually attempting to conserve the place that gay citizens have traditionally occupied in this culture—that of the singular, marginalized, complete outsider? And if the very definition of being a conservative revolves around upholding long-standing traditional ways, then certainly the gay critic of queer marriage is the extreme conservative in this case, while the supporter of full gay civil rights is the progressive liberal, attempting to reach new horizons that may have seemed impossible to imagine even twenty years ago.

QUESTION 17: My question to you is simple, but the feelings that I have attached to it are eating me up inside. I have no one to talk to about this and I feel as if I am losing my mind. I am twenty-six, gay, and living in the rural Midwest where *no one* talks about it. I don't have any gay friends and am living hundreds of miles from any city. I have the overwhelming sense that every person I meet hates me because I'm gay. These feelings have me totally immobilized. Help.

ANSWER 17: Your question cuts right to the heart of the gay rights struggle. We have all had the myths and lies in our lives for so long that for many gay men and women it is a struggle to simply walk out the door each day. It amazes me how many gay Americans still live their lives paralyzed into total inaction by an overwhelming feeling that everyone in the world hates them. So many of us believe that everyone we run into is an antigay bigot. There is oppression out there in the world, but everyone doesn't hate you. I guarantee it.

Most of the people you run into each day don't care what you do with your life. I don't say that in a negative or harsh way, but simply as a reminder that others are generally as wrapped up in their own lives as we are in ours. But your situation is very real to you and, judging from the letters I've received, it is fairly common, especially in more rural areas, or cities and towns that haven't become gay-positive havens.

My experience has been that many queers who live in gay-positive cities and towns do not grasp, or choose to ignore, a very fundamental concept. They think—or try to convince themselves—that the struggle is mostly over. There is definitely a strong rural vs. urban tension in our culture.

I fully sympathize with your situation. First, you must reach out and find help. Today, not tomorrow or someday, but today, locate the closest gay hot line or group in your area. Make contact. Drive to a city if you have to. You must set about shifting your perspective. Get several referrals for gay-positive counselors. Please, do this now. You need to seek out supportive professional help. Do not view this as a sign that you are crazy, but instead as a desire to change your life. Everyone does not hate you because you are gay. But I understand why you might feel this way. It is rooted in the lies told about us in this culture.

It is so simple, when you are an outsider—a queer—to be on constant lookout for the hatred of others, to search behind every bush, waiting for the homophobe to jump out. I remember when I came out in the media that the mail came pouring in—letters by the tens of thousands from all over the country and the world—and in so many of the letters from queers, the first sentence was something like: I know that you must get tons of hate mail, so I thought I'd write you something positive. Thousands of letters started that way. The only thing was that out of every ten thousand letters, only one or two would be in any way negative; only one in every twenty or thirty thousand could have been considered hate mail.

But many queers have grown to expect demonstrations of hatred at every turn, because many times the experiences of our lives seem to demonstrate that this is reality. But if we are to reclaim our true wholeness—as queers, as citizens, as humans, as dancing spirits—we will need to make a shift in thinking. It may be the most radical shift any of us makes in this lifetime. The change involves living as if we have every right to be here.

My highest hope for your situation is that you find a gay-positive counselor and a group of supportive friends who will help you through this situation which has you in such severe paralysis.

QUESTION 18: I attend a small college in the South. You spoke here a couple of years ago and I know that your speech raised a great deal of controversy on campus. After your appearance, I began to deal with the fact that I was gay. I had been pushing this knowledge away for a few years, thinking that if I just did the right things it might go away. I confided in one of my older sisters (she was twenty-two when I was eighteen) three years ago and she was very judgmental. She told me that I had to go speak with our minister and that if I didn't she'd tell my mother and daddy that I was a homosexual. So I went to our pastor. That's where my question comes in. I wanted to ask you this when you were at my school, but feared that I would be seen as gay if I asked a question. So, now I'm writing instead.

My question involves some group that my pastor described when I told him that I thought I might be gay. He said that this group was a bunch of men who went around having sex with boys and that would be what I'd eventually become if I didn't repent. He said that their slogan was, "Sex before eight, before it's too late," and that they always marched in the gay rights parades and that most homosexuals were that way. Of course, I've since begun to learn otherwise. The only thing is that there is a priest here on campus who is saying many of the same things. He is the religious representative of a group on campus trying to block the formation of a gay and lesbian support line—you know, a hot line for outreach, suicide intervention, and that sort of thing. How should I respond to this man's speeches? Many of my straight friends are beginning to ask me if he's right. I'm not sure what to tell them. I've worked so hard on accepting myself that I haven't given much thought to responding to these kinds of questions.

ANSWER 18: To begin, I want to say how proud I am that you've begun the process toward integrating your gayness into your life. I know that this may be difficult for you to believe, but I think that your instincts to confide in your sister were on target. Remember that she was raised with the same lies that you were, when it comes to all things gay. You had a few years to think about how being gay affected your life; chances are great that even if your sister had a notion that you were gay, it still wasn't a direct issue for her. In other words, she was once removed from the issue that affected your life directly; dealing with it meant a lot more to you than it did to her. Your mental processing was far more active than hers would have been and you probably moved past the myths a great deal more quickly. Have you ever spoken with her about it again? Have you tried to help her with the issues? Did you tell her about your negative experience with your pastor? You know, since it was a few years ago, she may have made some adjustments in her thinking. You've evolved, perhaps she has too.

What is the rest of your family situation like now? I would encourage you to peacefully, prayerfully look at where your family issues rest and think about how they can be better. I know that in the culture where you live this is one of the most difficult issues to deal with, but when you are really ready, you could play a vital role in breaking down the myths and lies for your entire family, having an impact that would last generations.

Now about this issue with the pastor and the campus priest: How do we deal with that one? I've been confronted with both sides of this issue at various lectures and in speaking with church groups. The whole thing revolves around one of the most insidious and slanderous of the lies that antigay forces tell about gay people — that we are child molesters by nature. Bigots can get away with exploiting this tremendous lie because so many gay leaders refuse to take a firm, unbending stand on issues revolving around one particular group.

The main group I'm talking about is N.A.M.B.L.A. (North American Man Boy Love Association), and even its disingenuous acronym makes an anger rise up in me, an anger that I have to work very hard to control. Thinking about what these men do to young boys makes me have to dig very deep into my spiritual beliefs, bringing to the forefront of my life everything I know about compassion and understanding.

I want to make one thing very clear: this group is nothing more than a bunch of child molesters. Period. What they encourage through their actions, their slogans, and their publications is older men enticing children into sexual acts. These men need psychiatric help, and lots of it. But also, and very essential to the point of your letter, what these guys do has as much to do with homosexuality as what men who rape little girls has to do with heterosexuality. This is not—I repeat—this is not a gay issue. This extraordinarily tiny group gets away with tying itself to gay rights issues because some leaders refuse to take a firm stand with them. This is most apparent at gay pride parades, where the child molester group always insists on marching—alongside other queer groups—under the N.A.M.B.L.A. banner. Some leaders use the very faulty reasoning that they should be allowed to march because all queers were once seen as perverts, so why should we discriminate against any group just because they are still considered perverts? This is one of the weakest arguments imaginable. It would be as if all gay murderers formed a group and wanted to march with pride in our parades. And just in case someone thinks that comparing N.A.M.B.L.A. to gay murderers is an exaggeration, I do want to point out that many adults who were molested as children feel as if a part of them was murdered.

This is a cut-and-dried issue. Gay leaders need to develop the backbone to say so too. We need to make sure that all child molesters get the help they need, but queer groups need to once and for all sever any and all ties to child molester groups such as N.A.M.B.L.A. Think about what you would feel like if it were your child that one of these slimy men was seducing and molesting. If it sounds as if this issue makes me extremely mad, you're right, it does.

I find it rather ironic that clergy are so quick to use this child molester argument still. There have been so many scandals about priests and other clergy taking sexual advantage of young boys and girls. I would think that their attentions might be focused on making sure that their colleagues aren't molesting children, instead of telling lies about millions of innocent people in order to mask their own naked prejudices. Let's face it: unless someone is in a severely fundamentalist setting, it is becoming more and more difficult to tell the truth and maintain antigay prejudice. Unfortunately, when the truth doesn't back up prejudice, many times supporters of an outdated way of thinking will resort to blatant lies, and they will lie in the name of God.

Your mission should be to live an open and proud life, as a good solid citizen. Live your life, with the same ethics, the same morals, the same sense of rightness, you would have if you were straight—just live it as a gay man. Remember that as you stand up to lies, you might experience emotional turmoil and ridicule. The truth is, however, that you are living the truth and that is more powerful than even the most insidious of lies.

Turn to your highest spiritual guidance—meditate, pray, look for hope. Remember above all else that in the situation on your campus, that phone line is an amazingly positive thing, one that could potentially save lives. What those who oppose this outreach are doing is misguided and wrong. Perhaps you can think of ways to reach out to them; perhaps their efforts aren't based on evil, but on ignorance. Remember the lies you were brought up with? So were they. Perhaps, with courage on your part, you can educate them. My sense is that too many times activists reject the potential for reaching out to perceived enemies in these situations. At least think about it. If you approach the leader of the group that opposes this outreach line, be nice, be clear on what you want to accomplish, be willing to forgive along every step of the way. In other words, feel your highest power fill your efforts with love and strength. You have the opportunity to stretch yourself here, to stand up against the energy that resists positive change. I wish you God's protection and strength.

QUESTION 19: I guess if you ask ten different people the same question you are bound to get ten different answers, right? Well, that is exactly what happened when I recently asked ten friends to help me out. Now I am going to ask you for yet another take on my situation. Here's the problem. I live at home with my family: parents, an older sister, and two younger brothers. I'm twenty and gay. Part of the problem is that my parents don't know that I am queer (although I have come out to my sister and she is one of the people who offered me one of the ten different opinions mentioned above). I do want to tell them, but it's a little scary to say the least. For the most part our family is quite open; we talk about everything. I mean, my parents did help my sister get on the Pill. I tell you that because although they really are "God fearing" in some ways, they are fairly liberal in others.

My sister tells me that I just need to have faith that they will be cool with it and that it is time to simply come all the way out. Different friends that have come out to their parents have had really horrible experiences that ranged from being thrown out of the house to the entire family being divided over it and remaining in constant discord. Both, I have to admit, are quite radical responses and I don't know that my folks would be that wigged out about it . . . but the chance does exist.

Another friend tells me that it was absolutely the best thing that he ever did even though it did change his relationship with his father (his parents are divorced). But he never had much of a relationship with him in the first place. That is part of my fear. You see, I am close to my family and rely on them. I just don't know how to handle this. I keep trying to come up with the definitive reason to come out to my family. Just one would do. So, all of that being said, do you have yet another solution to suggest?

ANSWER 19: I don't know about one definitive reason to come out to your family, but I can give you my own best twenty-five. Some of them may seem similar, but each reason offers a different way to look at the positive aspects of coming out.

1. By sharing this information in a positive way, you purge it of its negative connotation. You say and demonstrate that being gay is a positive experience, not only to your family, but also to yourself. We constantly reinvest in the myth of queerness equaling negativity when we shroud it with mystery or withhold revealing who we really are, treating our queerness as a dirty little secret.

2. Your family can get to know you—maybe for the first time—on a completely honest level. Once, my mom told me about my grandpa being very proud of my accomplishments in my sport. This was a couple of years before I came out to my grandparents. I wondered if he would still be as proud if he knew that I was gay. As it turned out his level of pride did shift once he knew about this part of me. His pride in me was based on a false illusion of who he thought I was. But holding untrue ideals never heal; they only separate.

3. You give your family members the opportunity to work through their own views of homosexuality. I don't care if a parent or other family member is completely rejecting and rigid, their view of gays will never be the same again. You have changed them through your honesty. It may not seem as if you have created a positive change, especially if you seem to lose the love of a family member you respect, but you have. Solid relationships can never be based on direct or indirect lies.

4. Coming out to family represents an amazingly effective form of activism. Think of all the lives you would impact if you told ten of your relatives, in a totally positive way, that you're gay. Now imagine that every queer you know does that; then imagine that every queer in America does that. How many lives would be impacted? How long do you think it would take for us to make quantum leaps of progress in queer rights issues?

5. Our families don't have the opportunity to support our issues if they don't know who we are. My parents never even concerned themselves with anything related to civil rights. It was only through my coming out to them, and then engaging in an ongoing struggle with the issues, that I was able to get them to look at the injustices I lived with on a daily basis.

6. You give your family the opportunity to get to know those who are significant in your life. In the future you won't have to pretend that your partner is a roommate, or hide your queer best friends because you fear that you might be outed by association. Again, how can your family really know you if they don't know those who are important to you?

7. You get to truly learn about unconditional love. If you are willing to hang in there—no matter how difficult it may seem—you'll eventually learn who really accepts you for who you are and who doesn't. Which family members want to really know you? Which only want to know an illusion of you?

8. There is every possibility that you can get family members to look hard at other long-held prejudices. It's much harder to hate others who are different if you are related to someone who turns out to be different from the rest of the family.

9. You bring to the forefront issues that could lie dormant forever. If you are coming from a place of pure self-love, a place where you respect yourself and your rightful place in the universe, then which would you rather have: a long-standing subterfuge regarding your personal life, accompanied by a superficial family relationship? Or an honest—even if interrupted—open relationship with your family?

10. You have the ability to break any cycles of antigay bigotry that might continue in your family. Even in otherwise enlightened families, the coming out of one member can bring to the surface underlying prejudices. The strongest example I can think of was an acquaintance whose father and mother were active in several civil liberties causes, but still were rejecting when their own daughter came out to them. With time and patience they were able to work through the issues and everyone was able to grow from the experience.

11. You can break the cycle of antigay mythology in younger family members. With each passing generation, we make incremental progress toward a just society. What passed for justice a hundred years ago might well be considered barbaric and unacceptable today. Those changes came about because new generations were willing to challenge old, outdated belief systems.

12. You'll never again have to worry if a TV camera happens to catch you at or in the local gay rights parade and your parents see you on the evening news. Even if they don't like it, it won't be a surprise. Just kidding . . . sort of. Seriously though, coming out makes you free of one very strong secret. So you can cross "getting caught on the evening news" off your list of concerns, including not worrying about the potential for a parent to see you kissing a boyfriend or coming out of a gay bar, or find a gay-positive magazine or book lying around in your room.

13. By taking control of your information—by coming out yourself and not waiting until a well-meaning (or perhaps mean-spirited) relative or friend discloses for you—the power to create a more positive situation rests with you. If you don't think that a relative or friend could or would ever out you (even unintentionally), you're probably fooling yourself.

14. Most likely they already know that you're queer. They might be in deep denial, but most of the time—at some point, perhaps years after the coming out—family members will admit that they knew even before you told them.

15. Friends come and go, but family has the potential to be a lifelong connection into the world.

16. You will develop potentially powerful connections with your siblings (if you aren't an only child, that is). Those sibling relationships can become strong lifetime connections, even if you only connect every once in a while. When you've been honest the door is open to more honest connections.

17. Sometimes because of being closeted to the birth family, a person spends so much energy building up a family of creation or choice—and in some cases this may be the only family that someone ever knows—that this effort substitutes for building stronger bonds with his or her birth family.

18. If you stay closeted to your family, you will cheat yourself out of the experience of lifelong and honest relationships with nieces and nephews.

19. By not coming out you participate in homophobia by omission. You participate in saying that being queer is a shameful experience and that coming out is a sharing of negative information. You deny your family the ability to love you for who you are.

20. When you deny the truth, you deny your own soul's growth. When you live with truth in all your relationships, you allow your soul to stretch its former boundaries.

21. If you've come out to your family and are on the road to creating a healthy, honest relationship with them, you can act as a sounding board and role model for your queer friends who haven't yet taken the leap. You might be surprised how much your friends want and need your help.

22. By coming out to family, you build a foundation of self-love, supporting who you are and how you live. The coming-out process helps you to truly accept yourself. Coming out to your family is probably among the most difficult disclosures you'll ever experience. Every coming out after that will seem easy by comparison, until eventually the process becomes second nature.

23. You will develop strong support systems for your life. For example, at some point you'll probably experience a broken heart, or some other tragedy. How can your family support you if they don't know you? While it's important to have your other support systems, your family may be able to offer some different perspective from your queer friends, on something as everyday as whether or not to continue a romantic relationship.

24. By coming out you become a role model of integrating sexuality into a full, well-rounded life. You turn your back on the myth that says all queers must be forever cut off, living lonely, desperate lives.

25. By not coming out you participate in the greatest lie imaginable. You lie to yourself. You give yourself permission to live a dishonest life, hiding parts of yourself. You risk falling into the trap of living a life where lies come easily.

I know from your letter that your spirituality is important to you. I went back in and looked at my old journals from the time when I came out to my parents, years and years ago, and found a prayer that I said over and over to myself during the days leading up to the coming out. Perhaps you might find it helpful when you get to the point where you are ready.

Infinite Spirit,

I ask for Your strength to fill my heart. I am about to reveal to those whom I love this thing that You and I know I have held secret from them. I ask that I am able to tell my family that I am gay, in the most positive and loving way imaginable. I understand that I cannot control anyone else's reaction to this information, but ask You, Spirit, for help in making my own reactions centered and loving.

I ask for strength and guidance. Infinite Spirit, allow this situation to unfold in ways that contribute to the highest outcome, a healing, the most blessed unfolding for everyone concerned. I give thanks for the love of my family. I give thanks for the gifts in my life. Amen.

AFTERWORD

When we are queer it sometimes seems as if the heavens have dealt us the most terrible hand. The entropic, pulling-downward nature of the universe dares us to stand up in the face of such an overwhelming curse. But if we have courage we challenge gravity, we push up against the weight of unquestioned submission to lies and false myths. We claim our place among the gifted. We are the gifted. We all are.

In the end, even when I still acknowledge my own ongoing struggle with the curse/gift seesaw, I know that when God made me gay, He gave me a mission of soul work, an advanced class in getting to the heart of the matter. My own individual calling—to be true to my own nature—has led me here, along a road cut out of densely forested wilderness by rugged pioneers. I give thanks for the work of pioneers, those women and men who kept on taking everything society could dish out, and who in one way or another kept turning their other cheek. Blessed souls preceded us. Blessed souls come after us.

We must continue on, doing our best to counteract the negative forces of fear and anger and cynicism. We must—each one of us—turn with even greater heart, even fuller spirit toward creating a loving planet, a loving nation, a loving neighborhood, a loving home. We must stare bigotry down, make it blink, through full commitment to justice for everyone.

I work each day to reject the barrage of messages coming at me that tempt me to be turned on by tribalism, separation, scandal, other's misery. I pray for strength to fight against this gravity, to go deeper and stretch higher. I look at my reflection in the mirror and see, where once a fragile boy stood, a man who loves his queer self, who wants others—gay or not—to also love their queer selves. And that is what I've learned.

After so many years as an activist, I have realized and put into practice the fact that activism's number one goal should always be a healing of the deepest, highest self. There is no peace or justice in a world ruled by self-loathing. Many balk at New-Agey terms, such as self-love; some cynics will call it narcissism, but nothing could be further from the truth. Self-love is what will heal our world.

. . .

I live on an island now.

It is a giant, tree-covered rock out in the cold swirling ocean and I have made a place for myself out here in what not long ago was—and in many ways still is—a wilderness; it stands seemingly separated, yet connected deep below the surface, and by the water; it's easy to forget that the water connects us too.

Others came before with oxcarts and axes; I came with a pickup truck and a laptop. I have a magnificent man in my life. Even if we left our wilderness home tomorrow, and headed back into the wilderness of an urban jungle, we have both learned that we are able to live anywhere. Pride comes before acceptance.

I am proud of my life, of who I have become. I struggled to get here. If anyone would have told me in high school that I would one day become—among other things—a gay activist, I would've laughed, then flinched and backed away, wondering how this visitor from the future could see what I thought I hid so well—even from myself. But it's there in the bones. Queer. From every lip that would have been an insult to my eighteen-year-old ears, but now it is a compliment. *Yes,* I say standing tall, *I am one of them, they are one of me.* The work of the soul flows out of the bones.

And now my soul moves on to other things. The work is not finished. I do not walk away in a literal sense, but it is time for me to move into a new phase. It is not a turning back, but a subtle shift. I have done my public duty. I retire now from this task to enjoy the fruits of my labor. I move on to live—quite simply— the life of a good, proud gay man, just going about his business. The tunnel opens wide and I am free to go about laying claim to the life I fought so hard to be able to have. I am of the Generation Queer: brothers and sisters who move together with love out of the darkness and into a paradise of our own creation.

000106

43170